60
THINGS I CAN DRAW

Dinosaurs and Prehistoric Animals

by Kaye Quinn

DERRYDALE BOOKS
New York

Copyright © 1990 by RGA Publishing Group, Inc.
All rights reserved.

This 1990 edition is published by Derrydale Books, distributed by Outlet Book Company, Inc.
a Random House Company, 225 Park Avenue South, New York, New York 10003,
by arrangement with RGA Publishing Group, Inc.

Printed and bound in the United States of America

Library of Congress Cataloging-in-Publication Data

Quinn, Kaye.
60 things I can draw, dinosaurs and prehistoric animals / Kaye Quinn.
p.   cm.
Summary: Step-by-step instructions for drawing dinosaurs and other
prehistoric animals.
ISBN 0-517-03566-9
1. Dinosaurs in art—Juvenile literature.   2. Extinct animals in
art—Juvenile literature.   3. Drawing—Technique—Juvenile
literature.   [1. Dinosaurs in art.   2. Drawing—Technique.]
I. Title.   II. Title: Sixty things I can draw, dinosaurs and
prehistoric animals.
NC780.5.Q56   1990
743'.6—dc20   90-38287   CIP   AC

10 9 8 7 6 5 4 3 2 1

INTRODUCTION

Drawing is fun! It can also be easy. Follow the step-by-step instructions in this book, and you will learn how to turn simple shapes such as circles, triangles, and ovals into fantastic dinosaurs and prehistoric animals. You will learn how to "build" a drawing, adding more detail at each step until your drawing looks just the way you want it to look. You will need a few simple materials to start.

PENCILS: It is best to start with a light pencil, so you can erase your marks easily when you add the final details. You can use pens, crayons, markers, and colored pencils to finish your drawing.

PAPER: Any paper will do–large, like newsprint, or small, like a piece of notebook paper.

ERASER: You will need a big eraser. The best kind is called a kneaded eraser–you can pull and stretch it to any size. It will pick up light pencil strokes and won't leave crumbs.

Now you are ready to begin!

DINOSAUR DETAILS

Some dinosaurs and prehistoric animals have rough, scaly skin. Others have bumps and knobs on their skin. Here are four easy ways to create these textures and shadows.

Short pencil strokes in the same direction will give your dinosaur rough or hairy-looking skin.

Small circles and short strokes will give a bumpy look to your dinosaur. A heavier line under each circle will make the bumps look like they're popping right off the page!

"Cross hatching" will give your dinosaur scaly-looking skin. Make short strokes in one direction and then "cross hatch" with short strokes in the opposite direction.

Short, curved lines will give your prehistoric animal a fur coat.

3

LET'S BEGIN!

Here are some basic instructions for drawing the creatures in this book.

Before you start to draw, look closely at the sample dinosaur picture below. Imagine a line that runs through the center of the dinosaur. We'll call this the "direction line." It shows the basic movement of the dinosaur, and acts as a "hook" on which to hang all the shapes that will make your drawing easy to do.

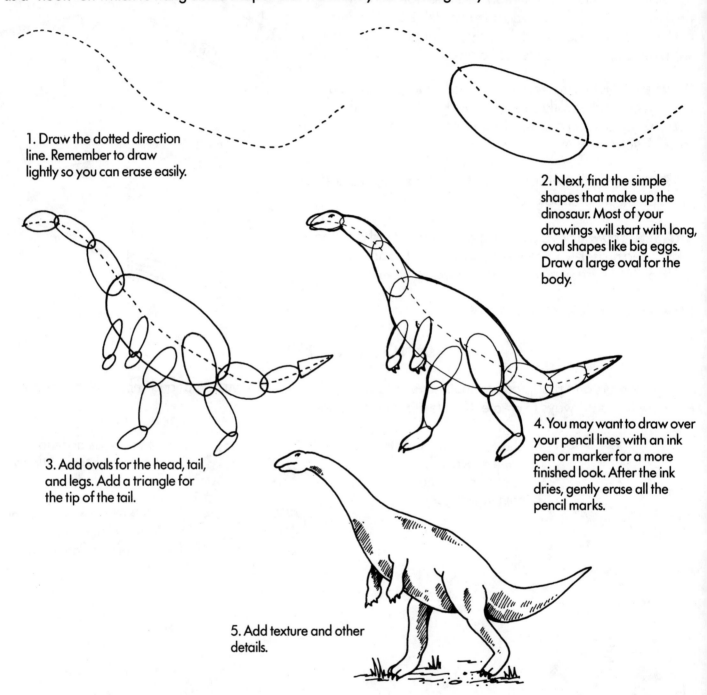

1. Draw the dotted direction line. Remember to draw lightly so you can erase easily.

2. Next, find the simple shapes that make up the dinosaur. Most of your drawings will start with long, oval shapes like big eggs. Draw a large oval for the body.

3. Add ovals for the head, tail, and legs. Add a triangle for the tip of the tail.

4. You may want to draw over your pencil lines with an ink pen or marker for a more finished look. After the ink dries, gently erase all the pencil marks.

5. Add texture and other details.

Once you learn how to build and draw the creatures, try some ideas of your own. Draw the dinosaurs in different poses and try putting two dinosaurs in the same scene. You can color your dinosaur and background any way you want. Don't worry if your dinosaur looks different from the sample in the book — it should. That means you are showing your own style. But most of all — HAVE FUN!

BAROSAURUS

Barosaurus (BAR-uh-sawr-us) was a huge dinosaur, about 90 feet long. Its neck was as long as 30 feet, which made it easier for the barosaurus to eat leaves off the tops of trees.

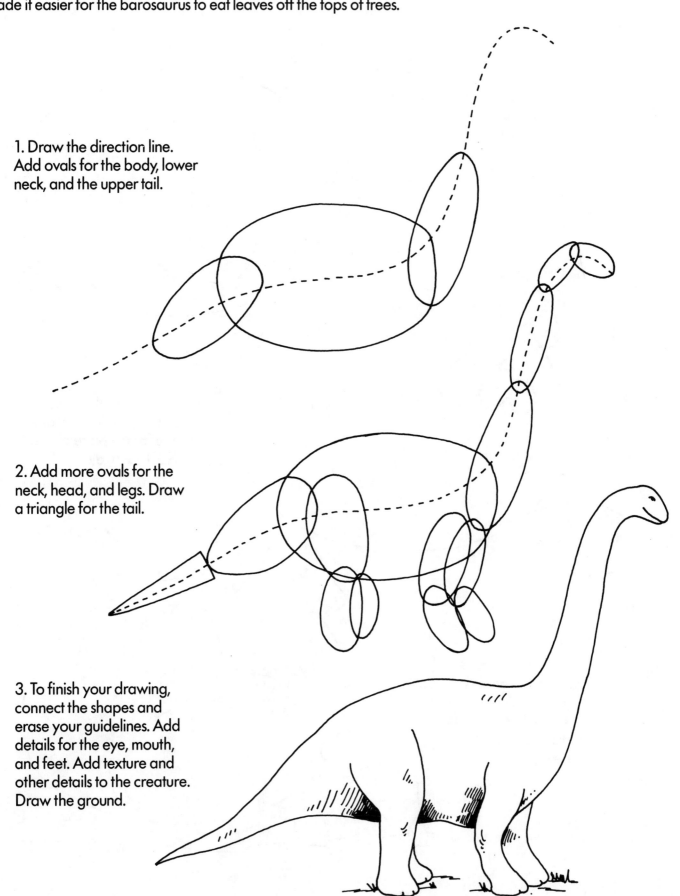

1. Draw the direction line. Add ovals for the body, lower neck, and the upper tail.

2. Add more ovals for the neck, head, and legs. Draw a triangle for the tail.

3. To finish your drawing, connect the shapes and erase your guidelines. Add details for the eye, mouth, and feet. Add texture and other details to the creature. Draw the ground.

DINOSAUR EGGS

The earliest reptiles laid soft-shelled eggs in the sea. The dinosaurs laid hard-shelled eggs on land.

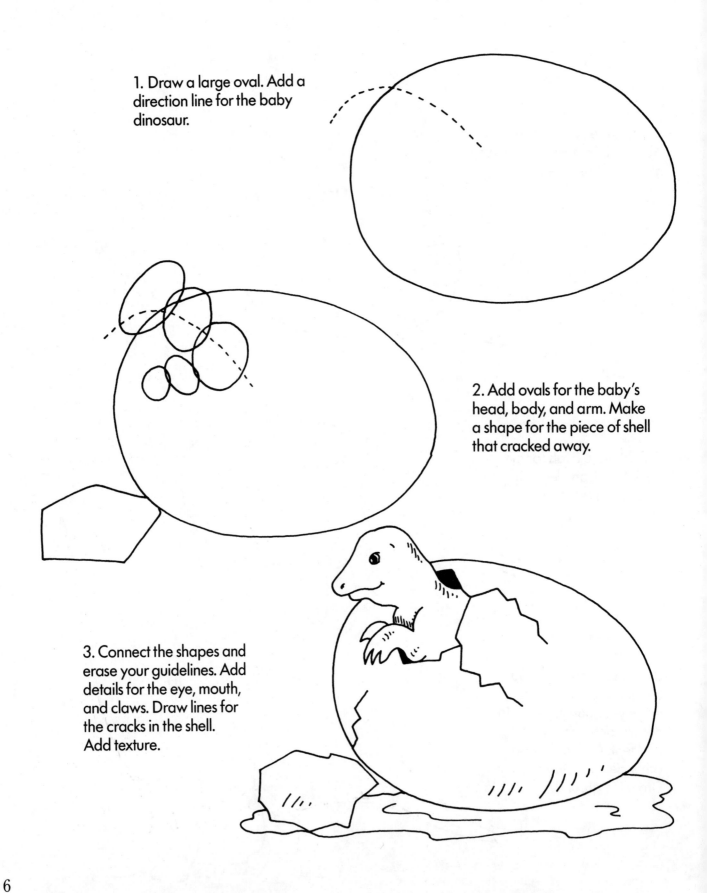

1. Draw a large oval. Add a direction line for the baby dinosaur.

2. Add ovals for the baby's head, body, and arm. Make a shape for the piece of shell that cracked away.

3. Connect the shapes and erase your guidelines. Add details for the eye, mouth, and claws. Draw lines for the cracks in the shell. Add texture.

BRACHIOSAURUS

Brachiosaurus (brak-ee-uh-SAWR-us) had a bony bump on its skull above the eyes. Brachiosaurus grew up to 90 feet long and weighed as much as 112 tons.

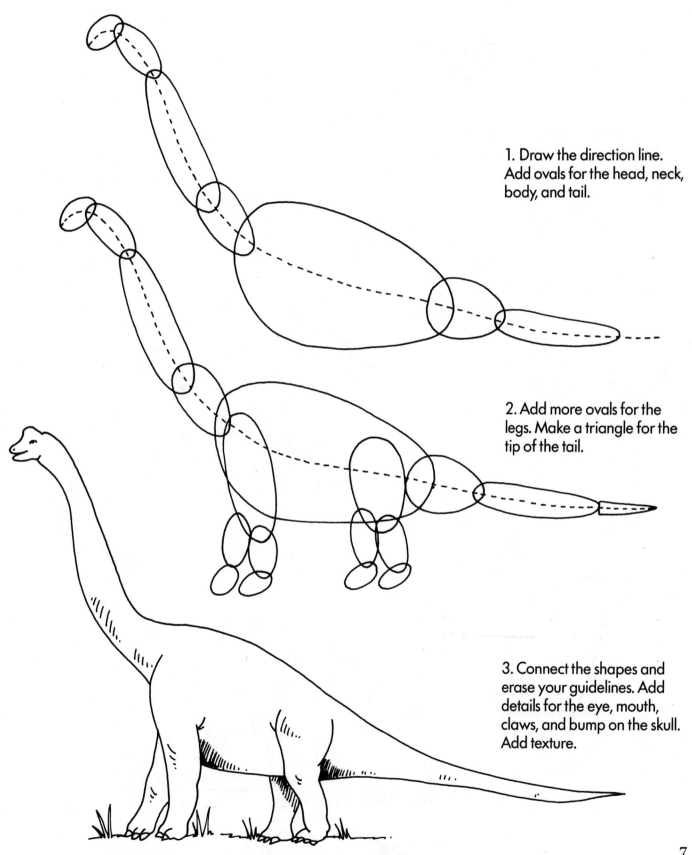

1. Draw the direction line. Add ovals for the head, neck, body, and tail.

2. Add more ovals for the legs. Make a triangle for the tip of the tail.

3. Connect the shapes and erase your guidelines. Add details for the eye, mouth, claws, and bump on the skull. Add texture.

APATASAURUS

Also known as Brontosaurus, Apatasaurus (ah-PAT-uh-sawr-us) grew up to 70 feet long and weighed as much as 12 large elephants. Apatasaurus had three claws on each back hoof. Each front hoof had four claws and one small claw on the back.

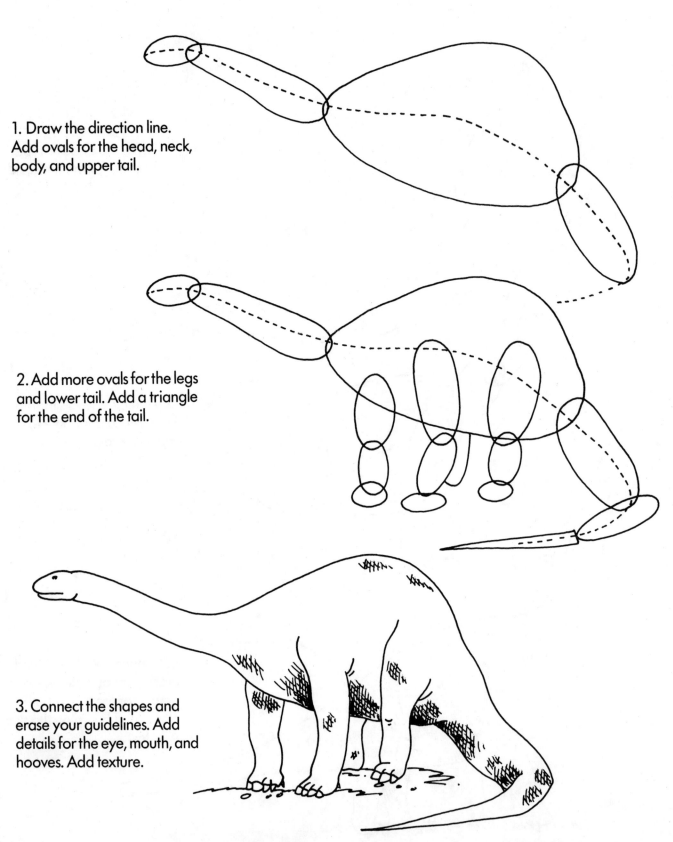

1. Draw the direction line. Add ovals for the head, neck, body, and upper tail.

2. Add more ovals for the legs and lower tail. Add a triangle for the end of the tail.

3. Connect the shapes and erase your guidelines. Add details for the eye, mouth, and hooves. Add texture.

ICHTHYOSAURUS

During the time of the dinosaurs, the seas were filled with strange marine animals. One was the Ichthyosaurus (ik-thee-uh-SAWR-us), which means "fish-lizard." It looked a little like the porpoises of today.

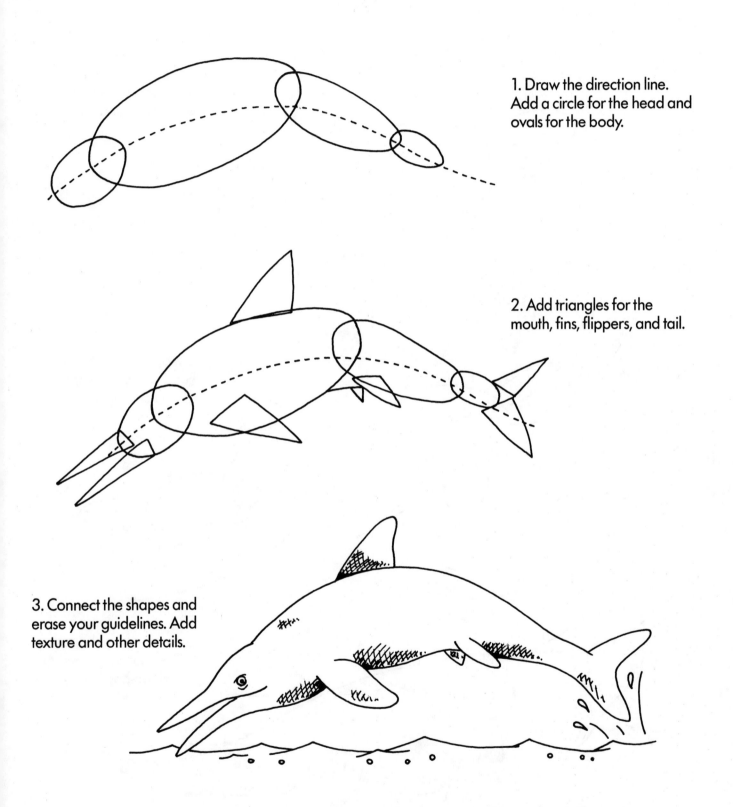

1. Draw the direction line. Add a circle for the head and ovals for the body.

2. Add triangles for the mouth, fins, flippers, and tail.

3. Connect the shapes and erase your guidelines. Add texture and other details.

ELASMOSAURUS

Elasmosaurus (ee-lass-moh-SAWR-us) lived in the sea with Ichthyosaurus. It moved slowly because of its heavy body, but it could catch fish up to 20 feet away just by stretching its neck.

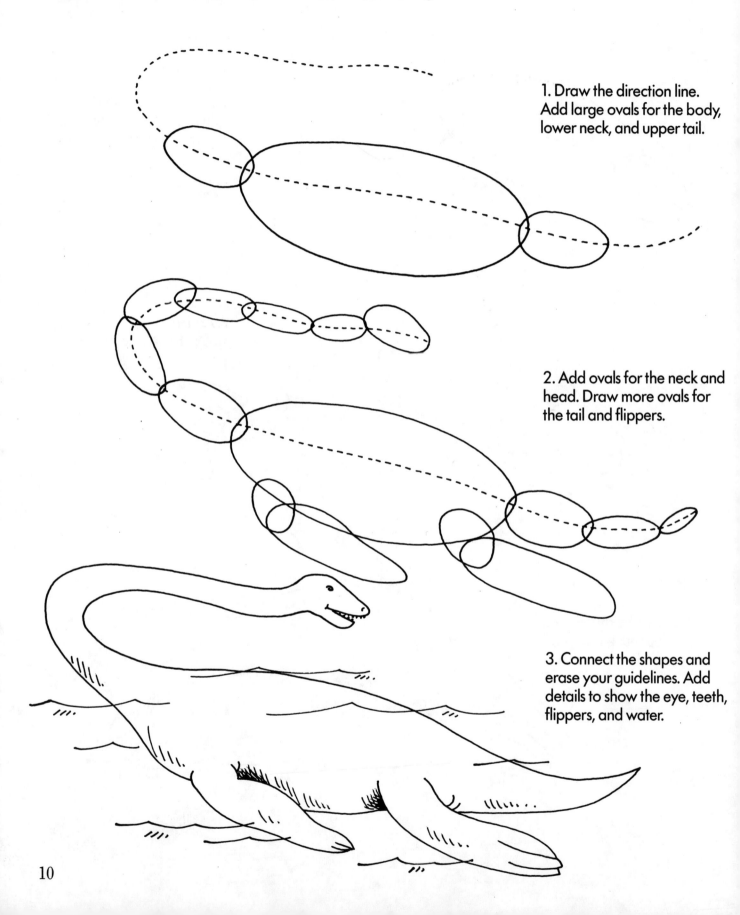

1. Draw the direction line. Add large ovals for the body, lower neck, and upper tail.

2. Add ovals for the neck and head. Draw more ovals for the tail and flippers.

3. Connect the shapes and erase your guidelines. Add details to show the eye, teeth, flippers, and water.

10

ULTRASAURUS

Probably the biggest dinosaur ever, Ultrasaurus (ul-trah-SAWR-us) grew to over 100 feet long and weighed as much as 150 tons. It had a second nerve center — a kind of brain — in its hip.

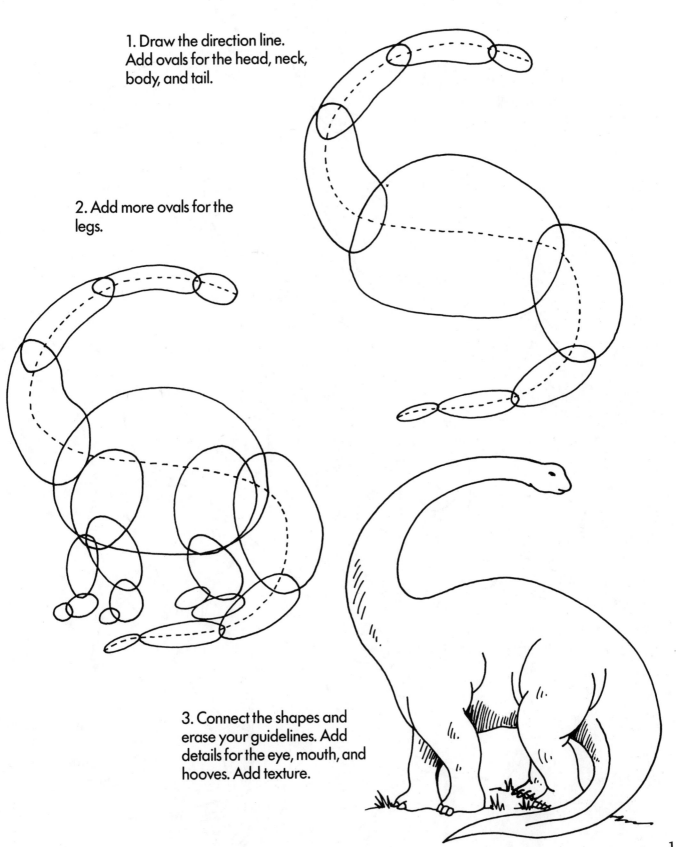

1. Draw the direction line. Add ovals for the head, neck, body, and tail.

2. Add more ovals for the legs.

3. Connect the shapes and erase your guidelines. Add details for the eye, mouth, and hooves. Add texture.

CAMPTOSAURUS

Camptosaurus (kamp-toe-SAWR-us) was a plant eater with a long, flat skull. It could walk on either two feet or four feet.

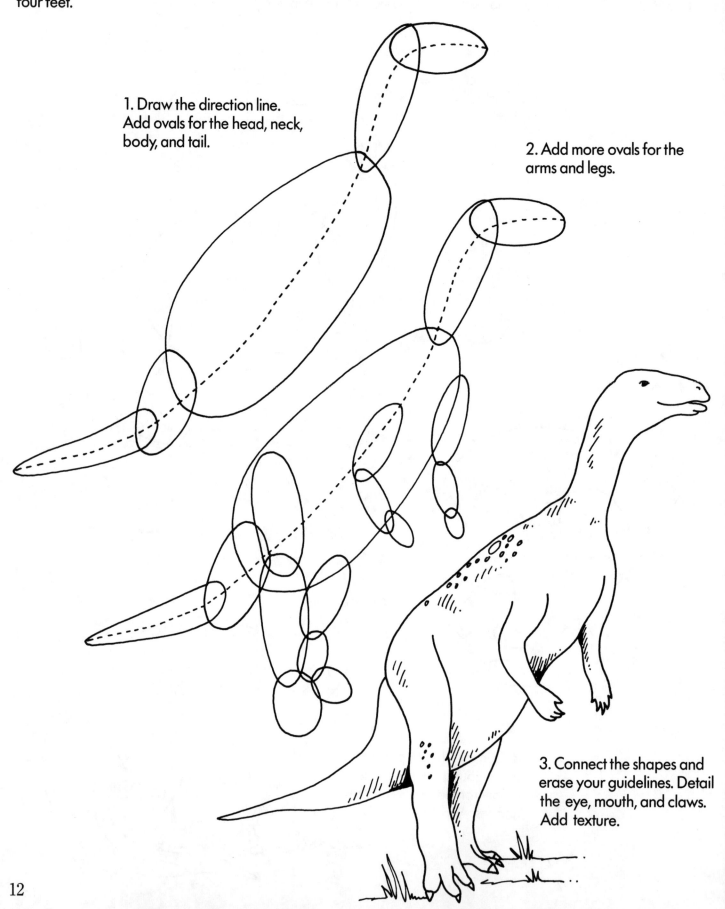

1. Draw the direction line. Add ovals for the head, neck, body, and tail.

2. Add more ovals for the arms and legs.

3. Connect the shapes and erase your guidelines. Detail the eye, mouth, and claws. Add texture.

12

PROTOCERATOPS

Protoceratops (proh-toh-SER-uh-tops) had a large, bony frill covering its neck to protect it from attacks by meat-eating animals.

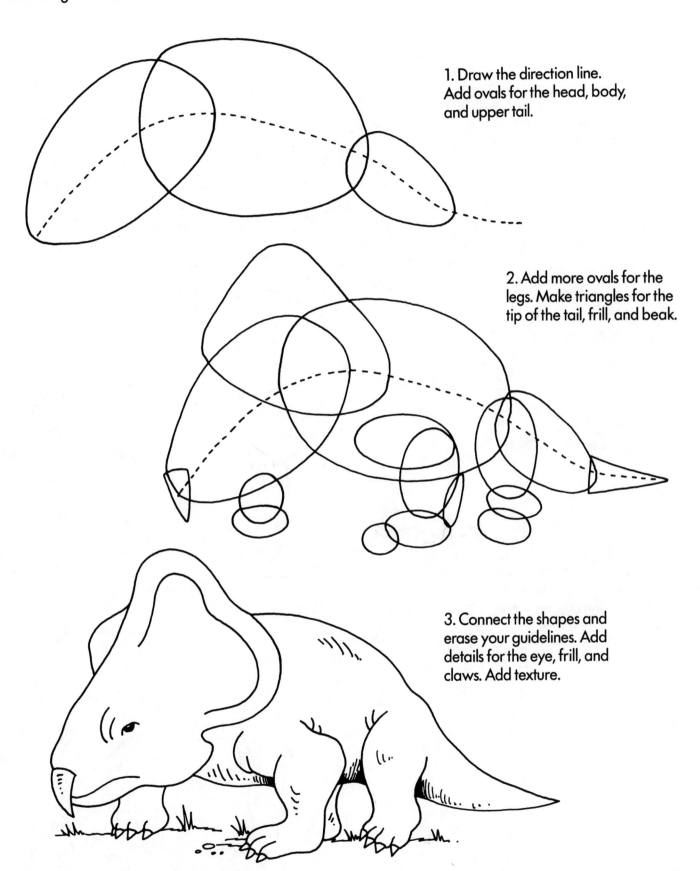

1. Draw the direction line. Add ovals for the head, body, and upper tail.

2. Add more ovals for the legs. Make triangles for the tip of the tail, frill, and beak.

3. Connect the shapes and erase your guidelines. Add details for the eye, frill, and claws. Add texture.

BALUCHITHERIUM

Baluchitherium (buh-LUKE-ee-theer-ee-um) often grew over 18 feet tall. When it stretched its neck, it could reach leaves 25 feet off the ground. Baluchitherium was the largest mammal to walk on land.

1. Draw the direction line. Add ovals for the head, neck, and body.

2. Add ovals for the legs and two lines for the tail. Add triangles for the open mouth, ears, and tip of the tail.

3. Connect the shapes and erase your guidelines. Add details for the eye, ears, and hooves. Add texture.

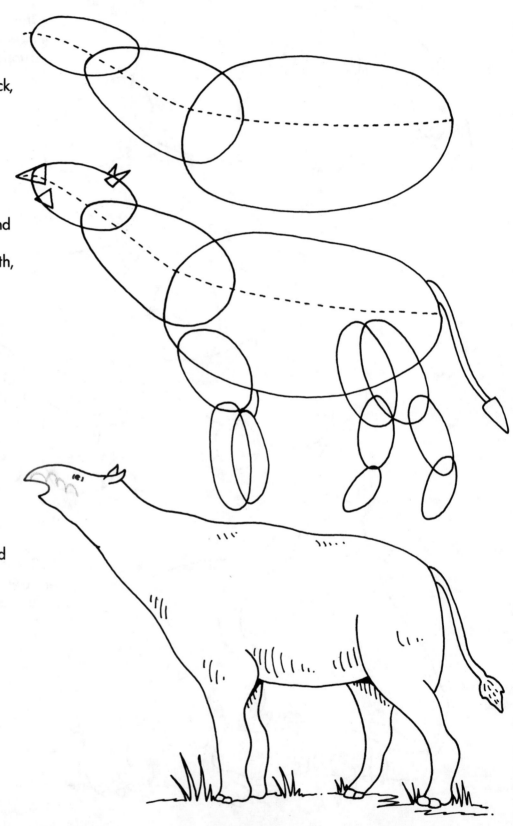

ARCHELON

Archelon (AR-kee-lon) was the largest turtle that ever lived. It grew up to 12 feet long and had a heavy, thick shell.

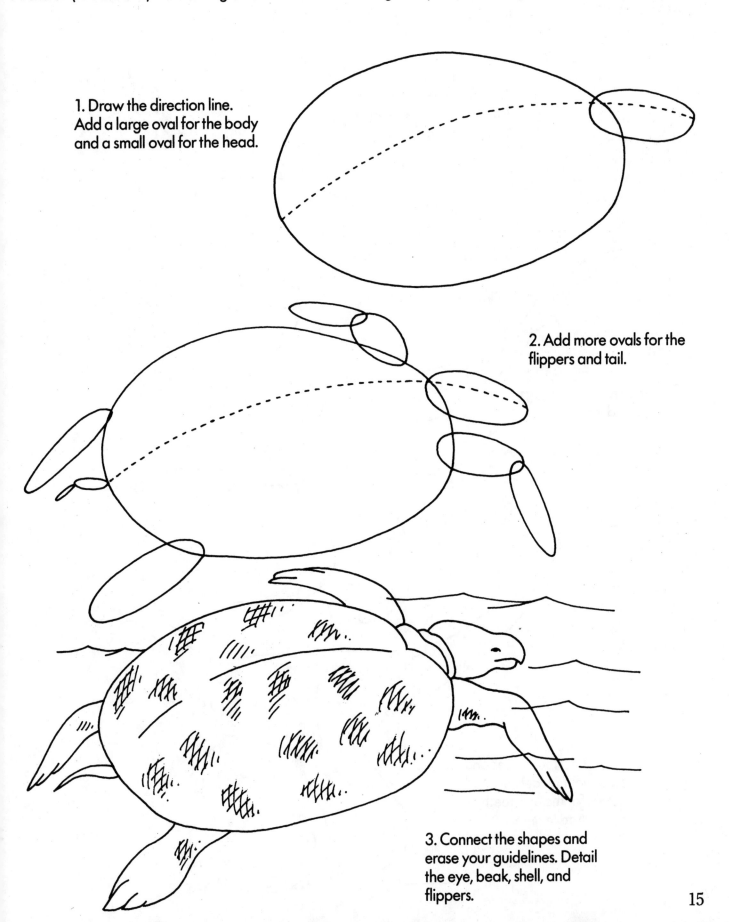

1. Draw the direction line. Add a large oval for the body and a small oval for the head.

2. Add more ovals for the flippers and tail.

3. Connect the shapes and erase your guidelines. Detail the eye, beak, shell, and flippers.

COELOPHYSIS

One of the earliest dinosaurs, Coelophysis (SEE-lo-fise-iss) walked on two hind legs, holding its long tail high above the ground.

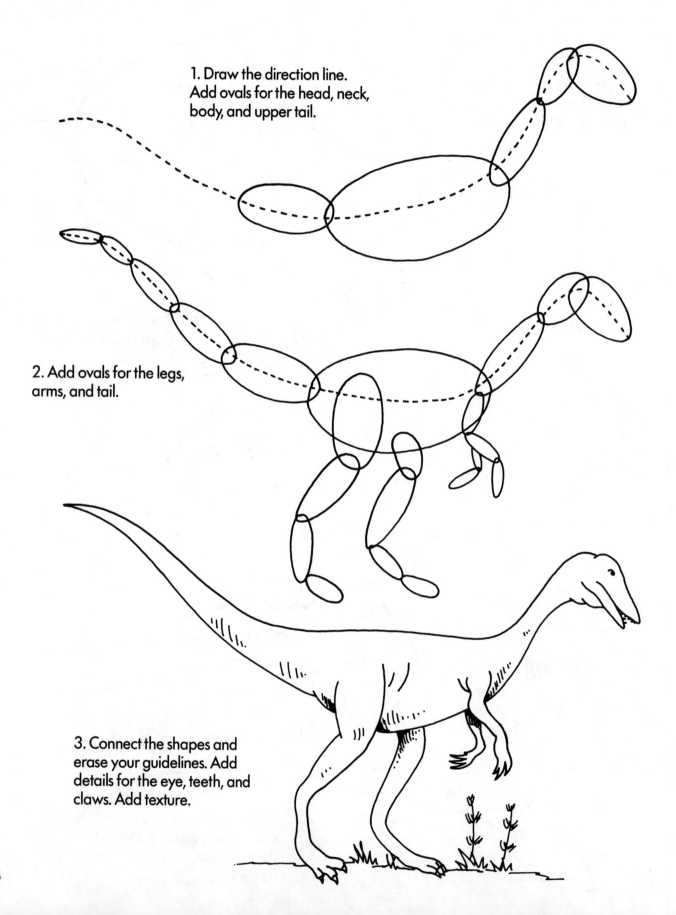

1. Draw the direction line. Add ovals for the head, neck, body, and upper tail.

2. Add ovals for the legs, arms, and tail.

3. Connect the shapes and erase your guidelines. Add details for the eye, teeth, and claws. Add texture.

ERYOPS

Eryops (ER-ee-ops) was a reptile that lived before the dinosaurs. Clumsy and slow, it spent most of the day sunning itself on swampy banks.

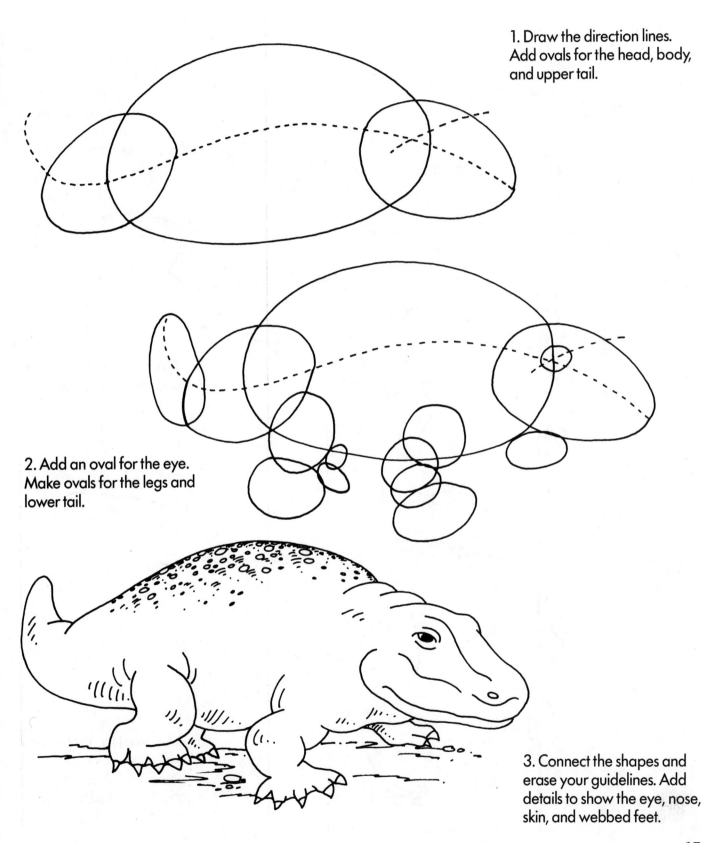

1. Draw the direction lines. Add ovals for the head, body, and upper tail.

2. Add an oval for the eye. Make ovals for the legs and lower tail.

3. Connect the shapes and erase your guidelines. Add details to show the eye, nose, skin, and webbed feet.

ORNITHOLESTES

Ornitholestes (orn-ih-tho-LES-teez) means "bird robber" because this dinosaur ate birds and their eggs. When Ornitholestes ran, it held its tail high to balance its long neck and head.

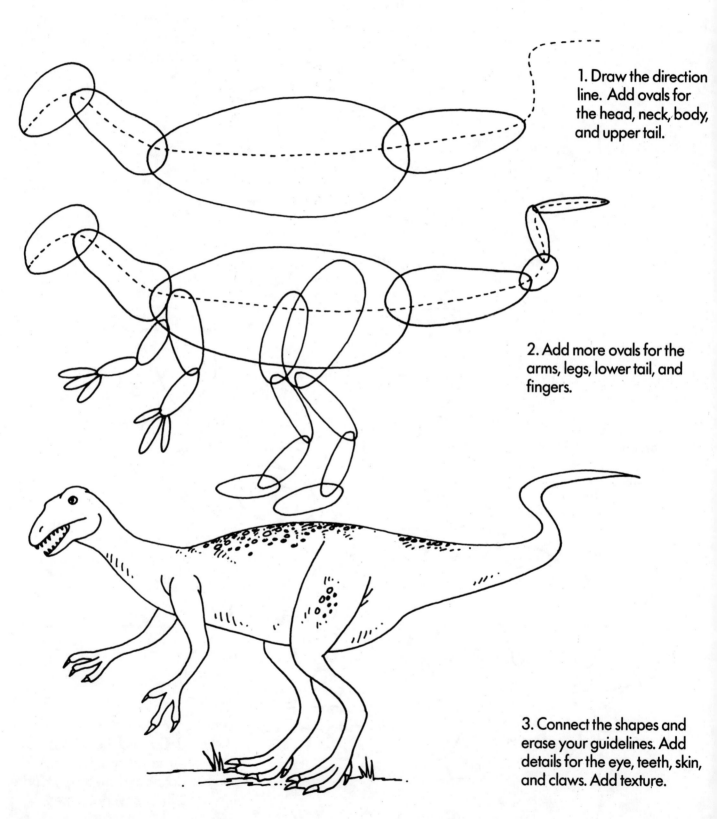

1. Draw the direction line. Add ovals for the head, neck, body, and upper tail.

2. Add more ovals for the arms, legs, lower tail, and fingers.

3. Connect the shapes and erase your guidelines. Add details for the eye, teeth, skin, and claws. Add texture.

18

LEPTOCERATOPS

Leptoceratops (lep-tuh-SAIR-uh-tops) was about the size of a large pig. Its mouth ended in a curved, parrot-like beak. A triangular frill covered the back of its head.

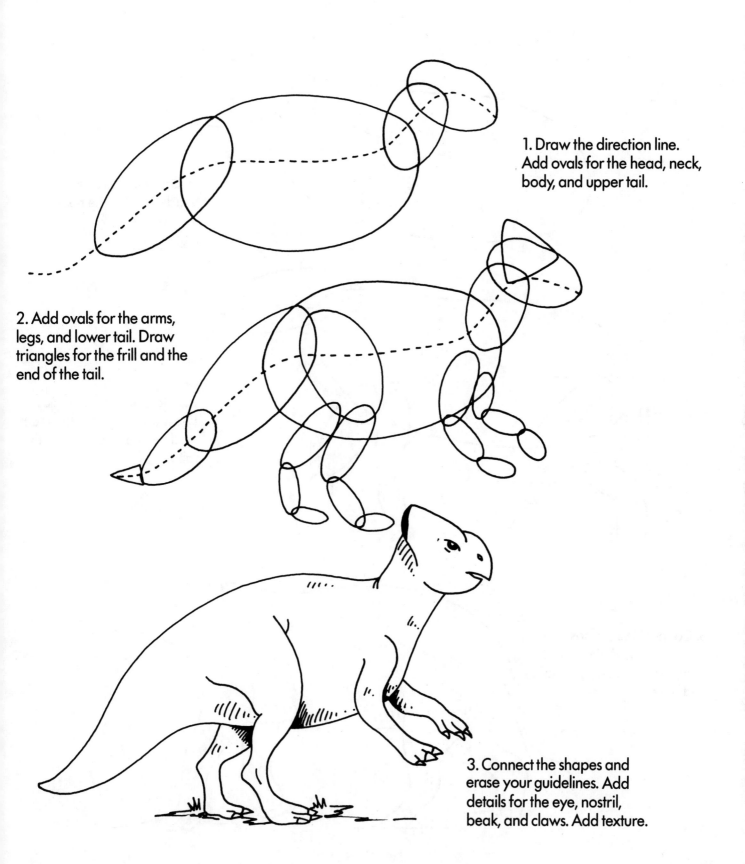

1. Draw the direction line. Add ovals for the head, neck, body, and upper tail.

2. Add ovals for the arms, legs, and lower tail. Draw triangles for the frill and the end of the tail.

3. Connect the shapes and erase your guidelines. Add details for the eye, nostril, beak, and claws. Add texture.

MOERITHERIUM

This earliest ancestor of the elephant was only the size of a large pig. The Moeritherium (more-i-THEER-ee-um) didn't have a trunk or tusks, but its snout had two long, sharp teeth on the end.

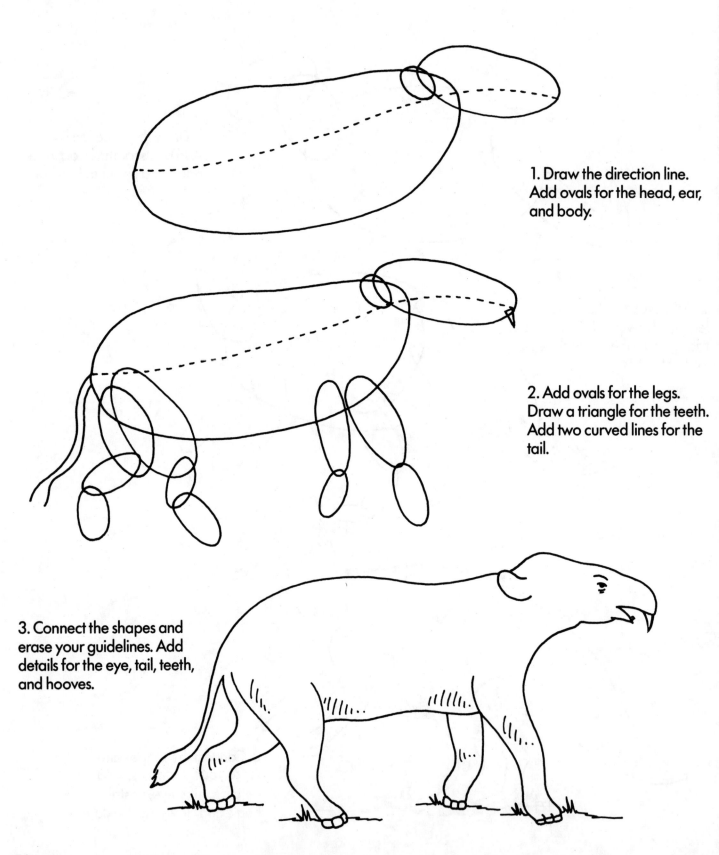

1. Draw the direction line. Add ovals for the head, ear, and body.

2. Add ovals for the legs. Draw a triangle for the teeth. Add two curved lines for the tail.

3. Connect the shapes and erase your guidelines. Add details for the eye, tail, teeth, and hooves.

MONTANACERATOPS

Montanaceratops (mon-TAN-uh-sair-uh-tops) was named after the state of Montana, where its fossils were found. It had a small horn on its nose and a bony frill that covered its neck.

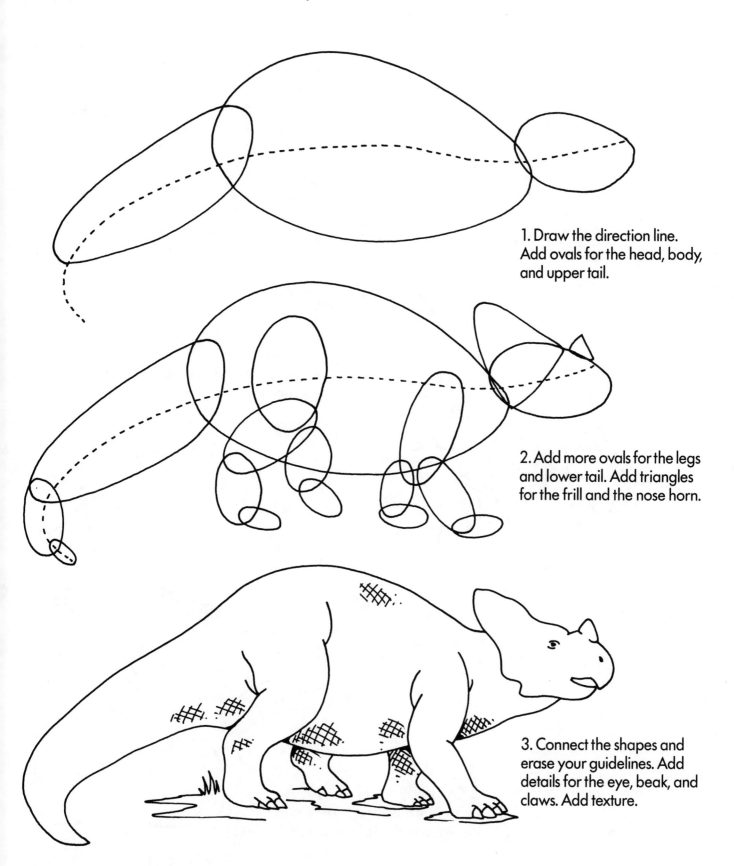

1. Draw the direction line. Add ovals for the head, body, and upper tail.

2. Add more ovals for the legs and lower tail. Add triangles for the frill and the nose horn.

3. Connect the shapes and erase your guidelines. Add details for the eye, beak, and claws. Add texture.

SEGISAURUS

Segisaurus (SEE-gih-sawr-us) was about the size of a rabbit and was able to run very fast. It was named for the Segi canyon in Arizona, where its fossils were found.

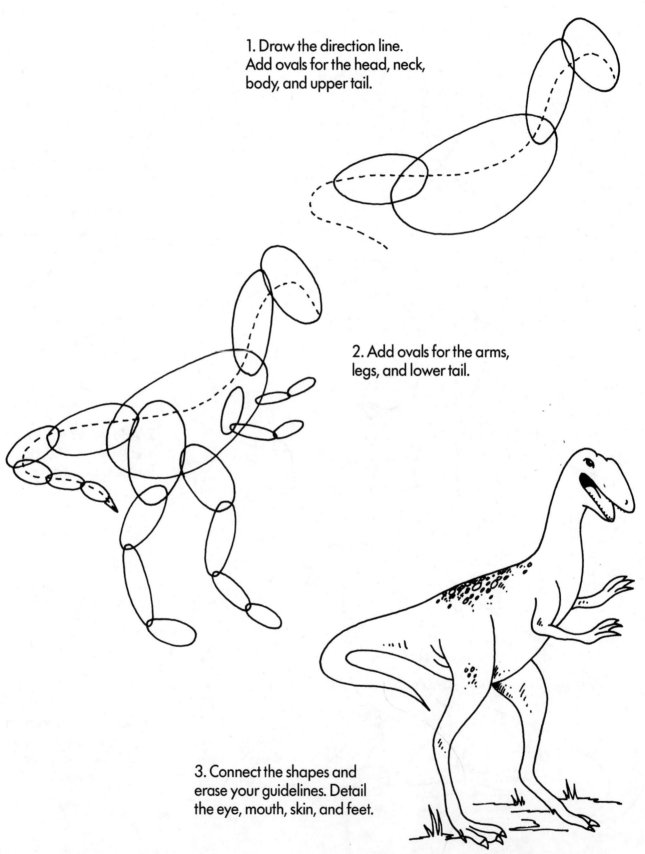

1. Draw the direction line. Add ovals for the head, neck, body, and upper tail.

2. Add ovals for the arms, legs, and lower tail.

3. Connect the shapes and erase your guidelines. Detail the eye, mouth, skin, and feet.

SEYMOURIA

Seymouria (see-MOOR-ee-uh) was an early reptile that lived before the dinosaurs. It was a descendant of the first reptiles that moved from the water onto land.

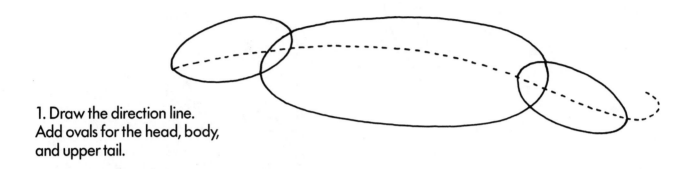

1. Draw the direction line. Add ovals for the head, body, and upper tail.

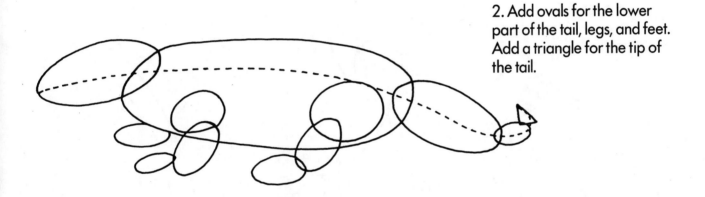

2. Add ovals for the lower part of the tail, legs, and feet. Add a triangle for the tip of the tail.

3. Connect the shapes and erase your guidelines. Add details for the eye, teeth, and claws. Add texture.

ALTICAMELUS

The word Alticamelus (all-tee-kuh-MEE-lus) means "tall camel." This dinosaur grew as tall as 18 feet and looked like a cross between a camel and a giraffe. Large herds roamed western North America a million years ago.

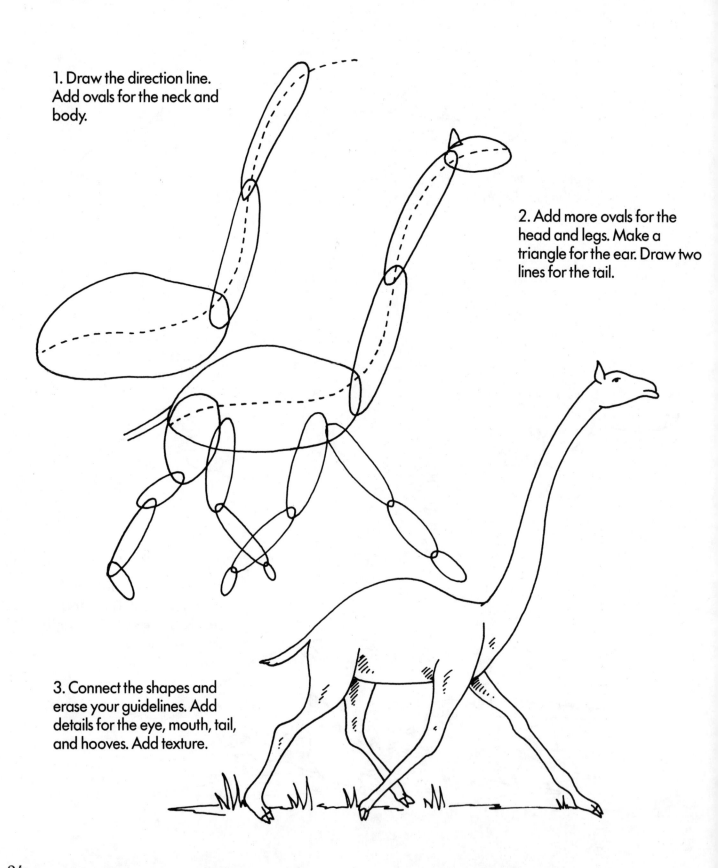

1. Draw the direction line. Add ovals for the neck and body.

2. Add more ovals for the head and legs. Make a triangle for the ear. Draw two lines for the tail.

3. Connect the shapes and erase your guidelines. Add details for the eye, mouth, tail, and hooves. Add texture.

ANATOSAURUS

Anatosaurus (a-nat-o-SAWR-us) belonged to a group of dinosaurs that were "duck-billed." Anatosaurus had broad, flat jaws and was a plant eater. It is also called Trachodon.

1. Draw the direction line. Add ovals for the head, neck, body, and tail.

2. Add ovals for the legs. Make a rectangular shape for the jaw. Add a triangle for the tip of the tail.

3. Connect the shapes and erase your guidelines. Detail the eye, jaw, and claws. Add texture.

MAIASAURA

Maiasaura (mah-ee-uh-SAWR-uh) means "good mother lizard." It is called this because scientists found its fossils in a nest with the fossils of babies. Maiasaura had a short bony spike above its eyes.

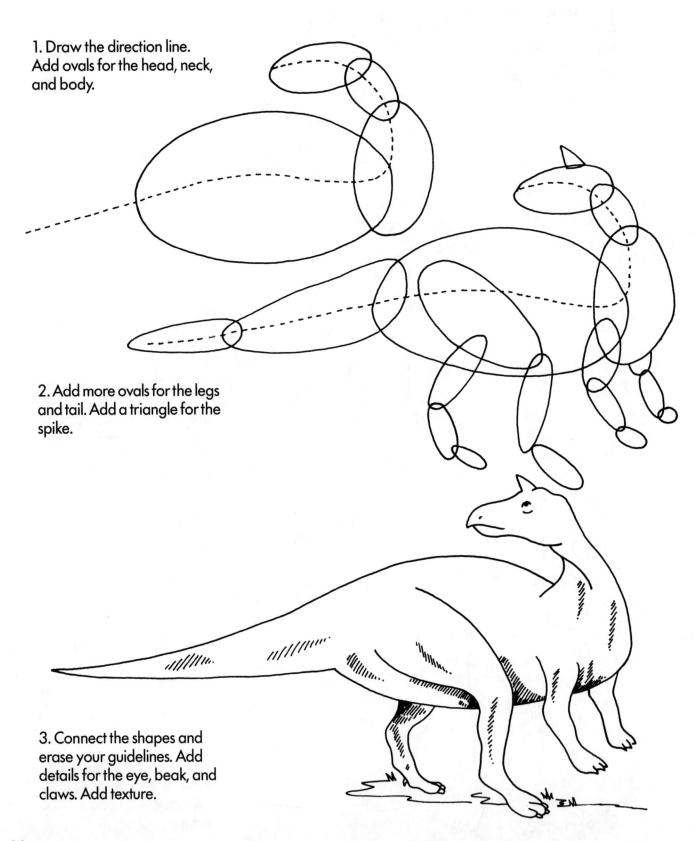

1. Draw the direction line. Add ovals for the head, neck, and body.

2. Add more ovals for the legs and tail. Add a triangle for the spike.

3. Connect the shapes and erase your guidelines. Add details for the eye, beak, and claws. Add texture.

MOROPUS

Moropus (MOR-uh-pus) means "foolish-footed." This animal had feet with long, sharp claws. Moropus looked sort of like a hairy horse. Its front legs were longer than its back legs, so its body sloped downward.

1. Draw the direction line. Add ovals for the head, neck, and body.

2. Draw more ovals for the legs and tail.

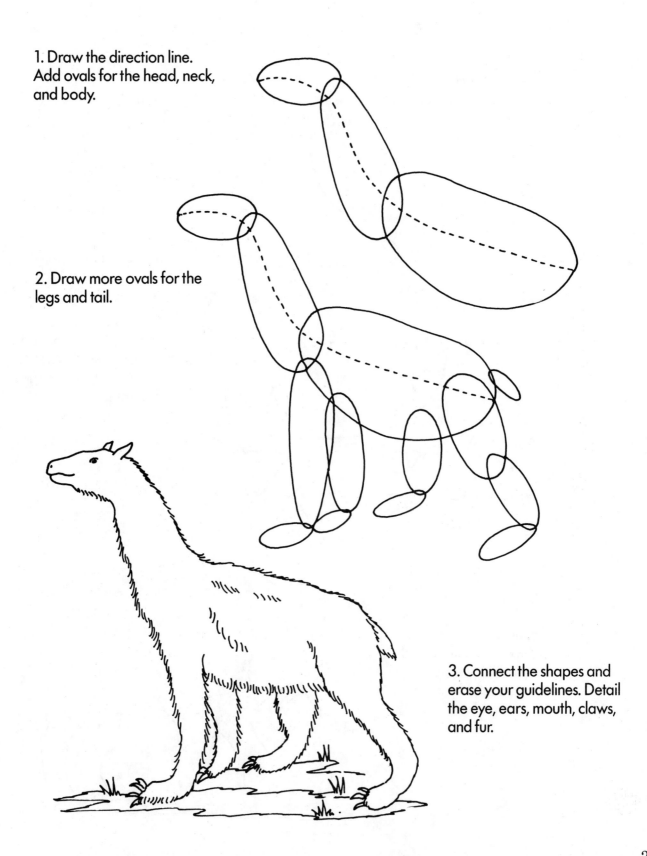

3. Connect the shapes and erase your guidelines. Detail the eye, ears, mouth, claws, and fur.

DEINOTHERIUM

Deinotherium (dy-no-THEER-ee-um) was an early elephant that lived about 15 million years ago. It looked like the elephant of today, except its tusks were curved inward.

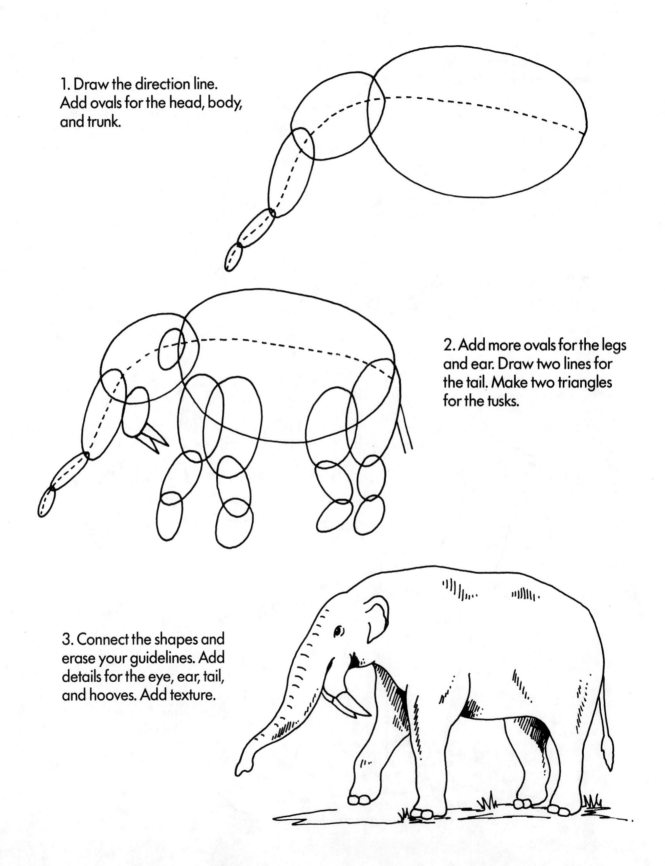

1. Draw the direction line. Add ovals for the head, body, and trunk.

2. Add more ovals for the legs and ear. Draw two lines for the tail. Make two triangles for the tusks.

3. Connect the shapes and erase your guidelines. Add details for the eye, ear, tail, and hooves. Add texture.

ANCHISAURUS

Anchisaurus (ANN-kih-sawr-us) was a plant eater with very blunt teeth. Because its bones have been discovered in groups, scientists think it may have lived in herds for protection.

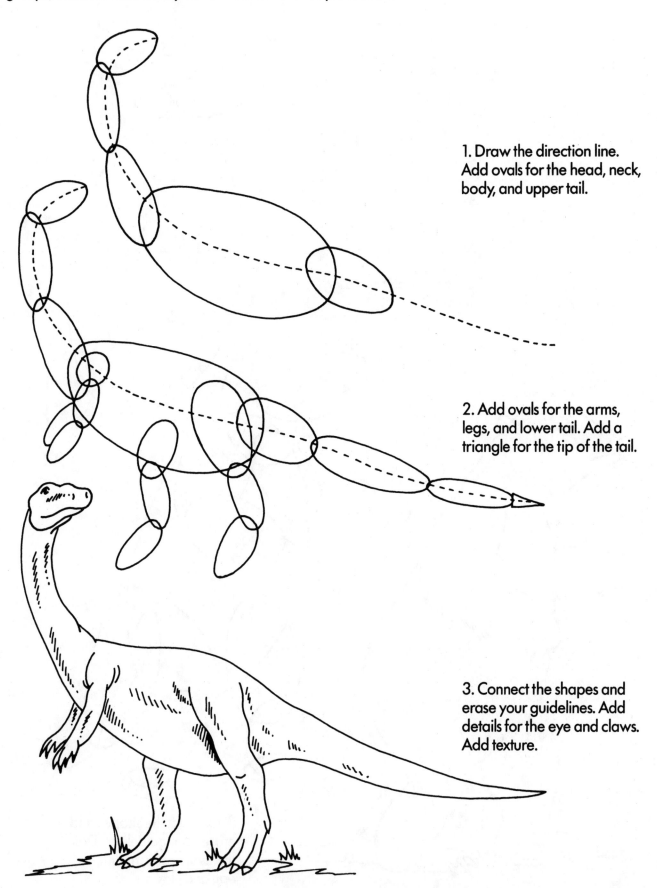

1. Draw the direction line. Add ovals for the head, neck, body, and upper tail.

2. Add ovals for the arms, legs, and lower tail. Add a triangle for the tip of the tail.

3. Connect the shapes and erase your guidelines. Add details for the eye and claws. Add texture.

MEGATHERIUM

Megatherium (meg-ah-THEER-ee-um) was a giant ground sloth. Clumsy and slow-moving, it had large claws to rake the leaves off trees and to protect itself.

1. Draw the direction line. Add ovals for the head, neck, body, and upper tail.

2. Add more ovals for the legs and lower tail.

3. Connect the shapes and erase your guidelines. Detail the eye, nostril, mouth, fur, ear, and claws.

DRYPTASAURUS

A ferocious meat eater, Dryptasaurus (DRIP-tuh-sawr-us) had sharp teeth and long claws. Its short arms were very powerful.

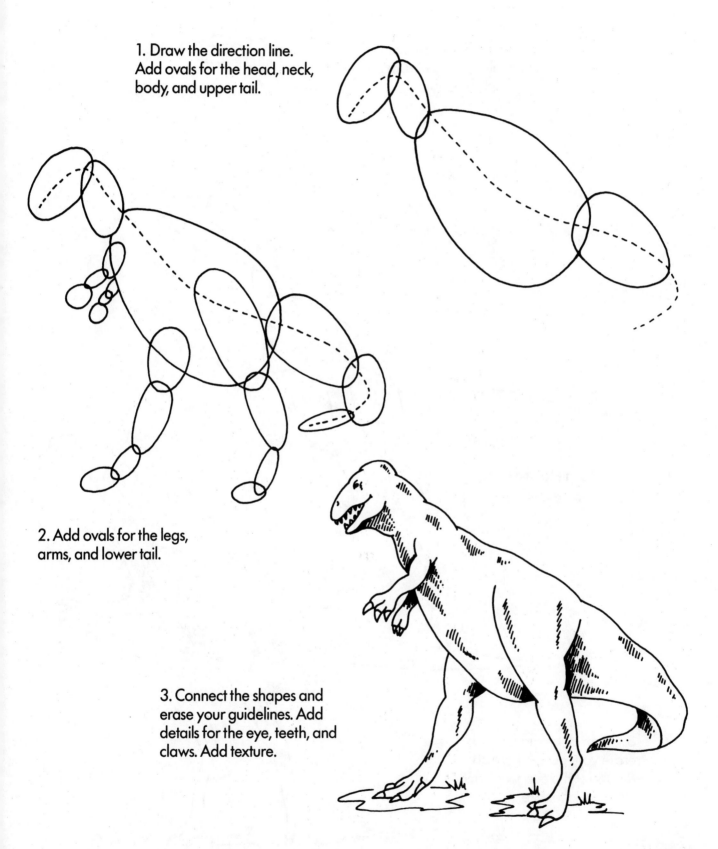

1. Draw the direction line. Add ovals for the head, neck, body, and upper tail.

2. Add ovals for the legs, arms, and lower tail.

3. Connect the shapes and erase your guidelines. Add details for the eye, teeth, and claws. Add texture.

COMPSOGNATHUS

One of the smallest dinosaurs, Compsognathus (comp-so-NA-thus) was about the size of a chicken. It was a swift runner and could catch lizards.

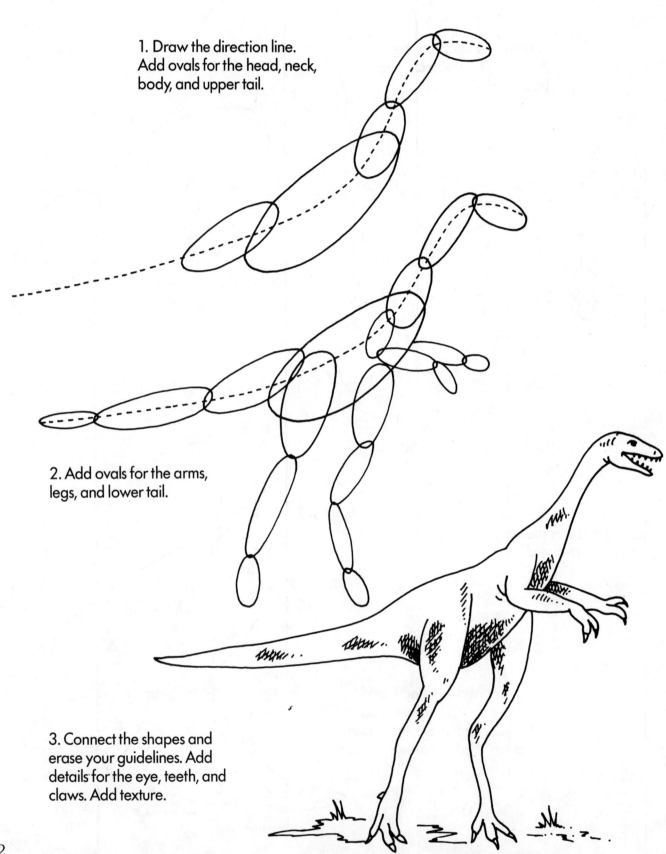

1. Draw the direction line. Add ovals for the head, neck, body, and upper tail.

2. Add ovals for the arms, legs, and lower tail.

3. Connect the shapes and erase your guidelines. Add details for the eye, teeth, and claws. Add texture.

CAVE BEAR

Scientists believe cave bears were hunted for food and for their fur because many of their bones have been found in the caves of early man.

1. Draw direction lines for the body and for the eyes. Add ovals for the head, neck, and body.

2. Add more ovals for legs. Make shapes for the ears and nose.

3. Connect the shapes and erase your guidelines. Detail the eyes, mouth, nose, paws, and fur.

WOOLLY RHINOCEROS

The huge Woolly Rhinoceros lived during the Ice Age. Its thick fur kept it warm, and its layers of fat were used as fuel when other food sources were scarce.

1. Draw the direction line. Add ovals for the head, neck, and body.

2. Add more ovals for the legs and tail. Draw triangles for the horns and ears.

3. Connect the shapes and erase your guidelines. Add details to show the eye, nostril, hooves, and fur.

PACHYCEPHALOSAURUS

Pachycephalosaurus (pak-ee-SEF-uh-lo-sawr-us) is sometimes called "bonehead." Its skull grew as thick as 10 inches. It had knobs on the back of its head and on its nose.

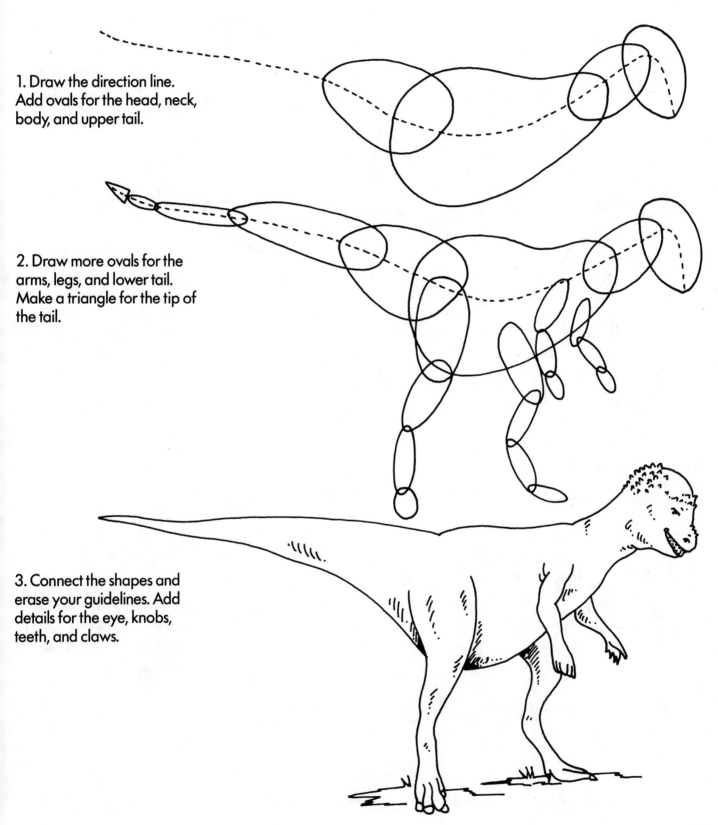

1. Draw the direction line. Add ovals for the head, neck, body, and upper tail.

2. Draw more ovals for the arms, legs, and lower tail. Make a triangle for the tip of the tail.

3. Connect the shapes and erase your guidelines. Add details for the eye, knobs, teeth, and claws.

DEINONYCHUS

Deinonychus (dine-ON-ik-us) was a fast and fierce hunter. On each foot it had a large knife-like claw that it swung back and forth to cut its enemies.

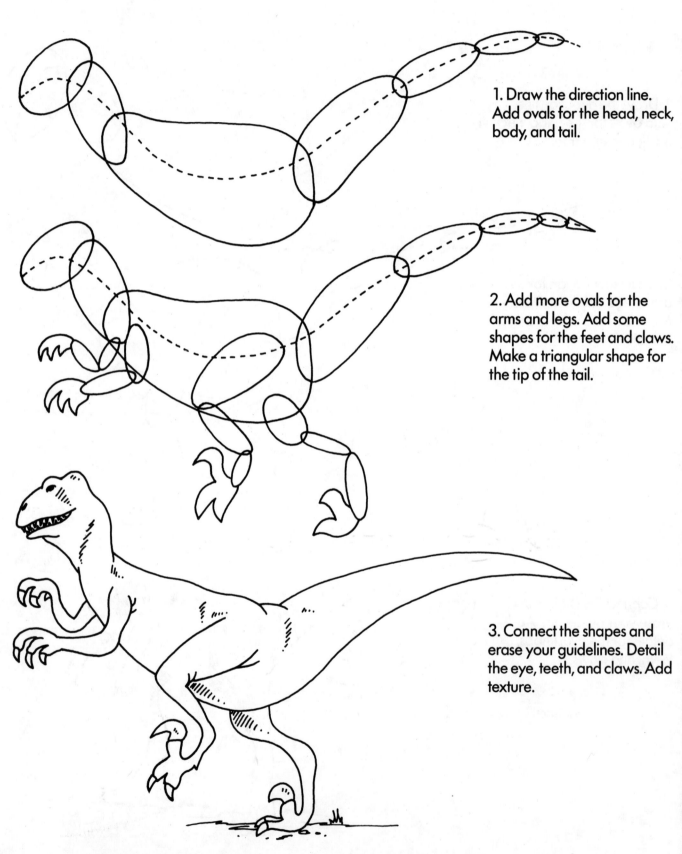

1. Draw the direction line. Add ovals for the head, neck, body, and tail.

2. Add more ovals for the arms and legs. Add some shapes for the feet and claws. Make a triangular shape for the tip of the tail.

3. Connect the shapes and erase your guidelines. Detail the eye, teeth, and claws. Add texture.

MASTODON

Mastodon (MASS-to-don) was an early elephant with long curved tusks and a furry body. It first appeared 25 million years ago.

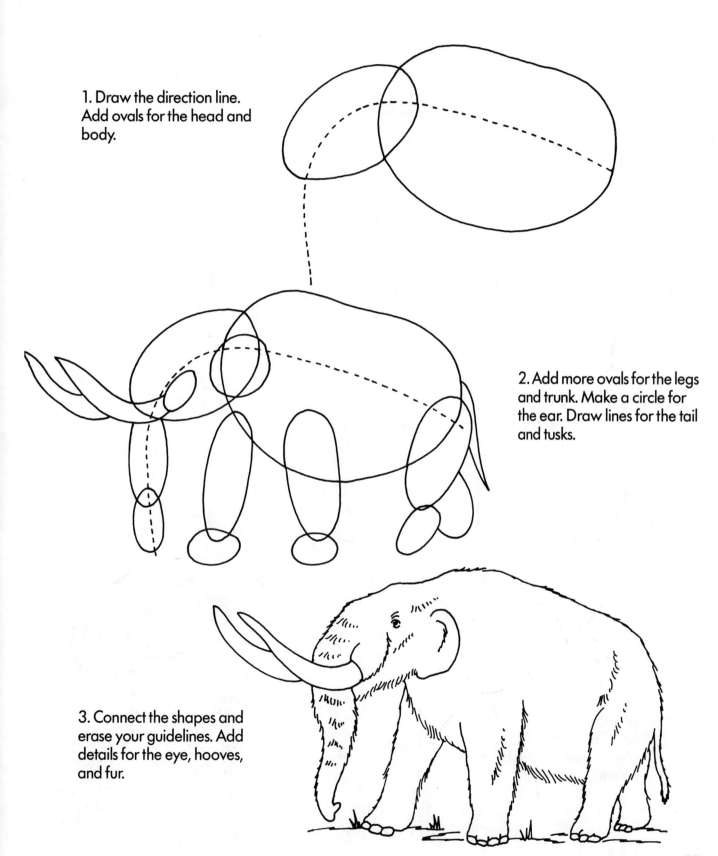

1. Draw the direction line. Add ovals for the head and body.

2. Add more ovals for the legs and trunk. Make a circle for the ear. Draw lines for the tail and tusks.

3. Connect the shapes and erase your guidelines. Add details for the eye, hooves, and fur.

DILOPHOSAURUS

Built for speed, Dilophosaurus (die-LO-fuh-sawr-us) ran on powerful hind legs. It had three long toes and one short toe. Its most unusual feature was its large skull with two bony crests across the top. Let's practice drawing the head of the Dilophosaurus first.

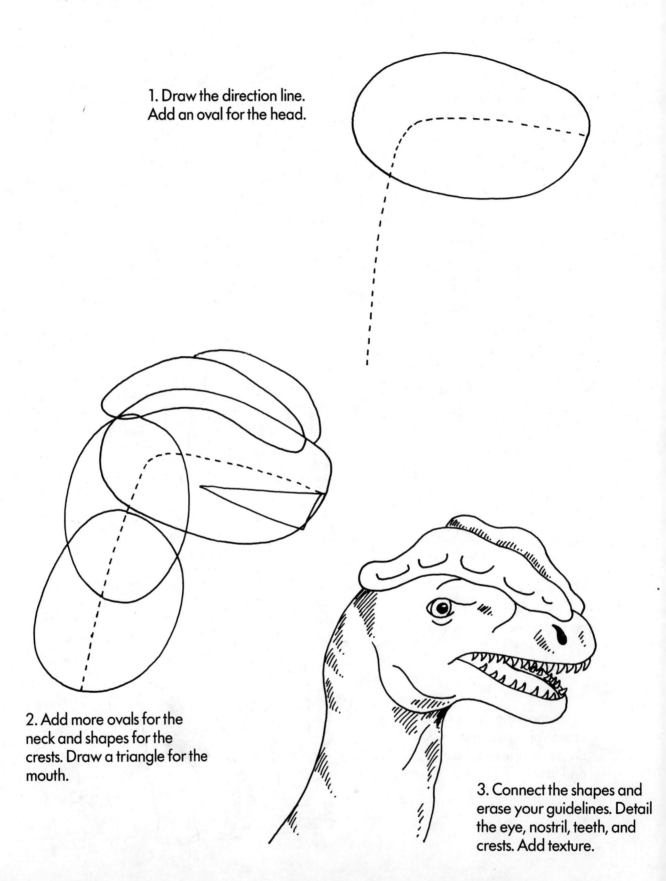

1. Draw the direction line. Add an oval for the head.

2. Add more ovals for the neck and shapes for the crests. Draw a triangle for the mouth.

3. Connect the shapes and erase your guidelines. Detail the eye, nostril, teeth, and crests. Add texture.

Now let's draw the full body of the Dilophosaurus.

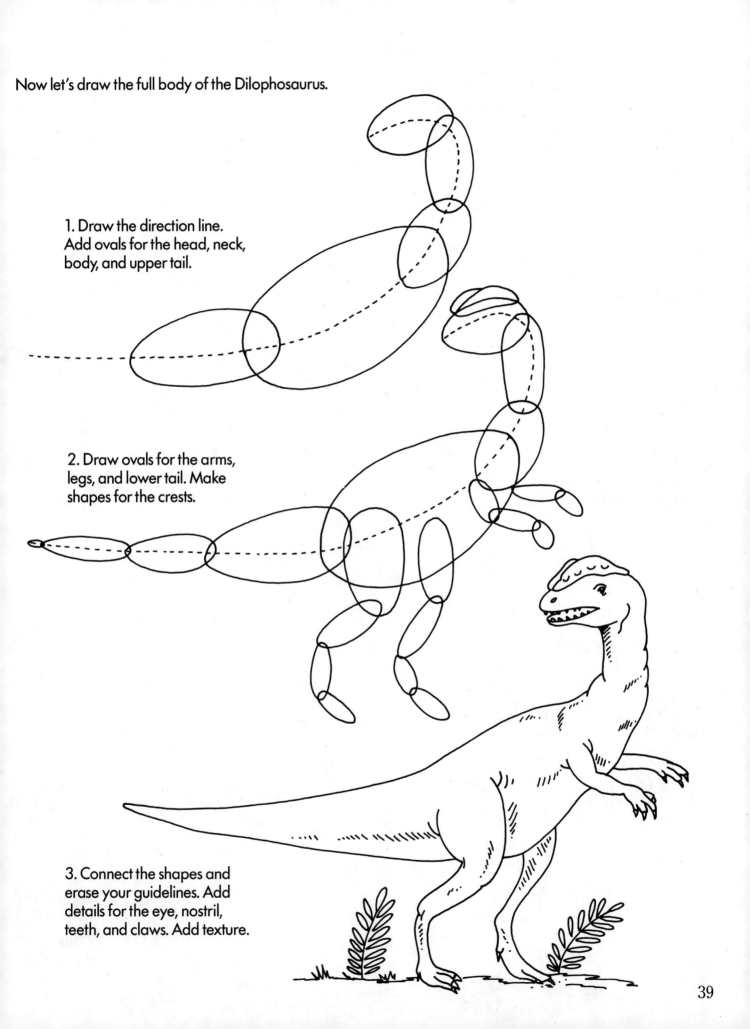

1. Draw the direction line. Add ovals for the head, neck, body, and upper tail.

2. Draw ovals for the arms, legs, and lower tail. Make shapes for the crests.

3. Connect the shapes and erase your guidelines. Add details for the eye, nostril, teeth, and claws. Add texture.

ACROCANTHOSAURUS

Acrocanthosaurus (ak-ro-KANTH-uh-sawr-us) was sometimes as big as 40 feet long. Its powerful hind legs were built for running. It had a row of spines along its back. Its name means "very spiny lizard."

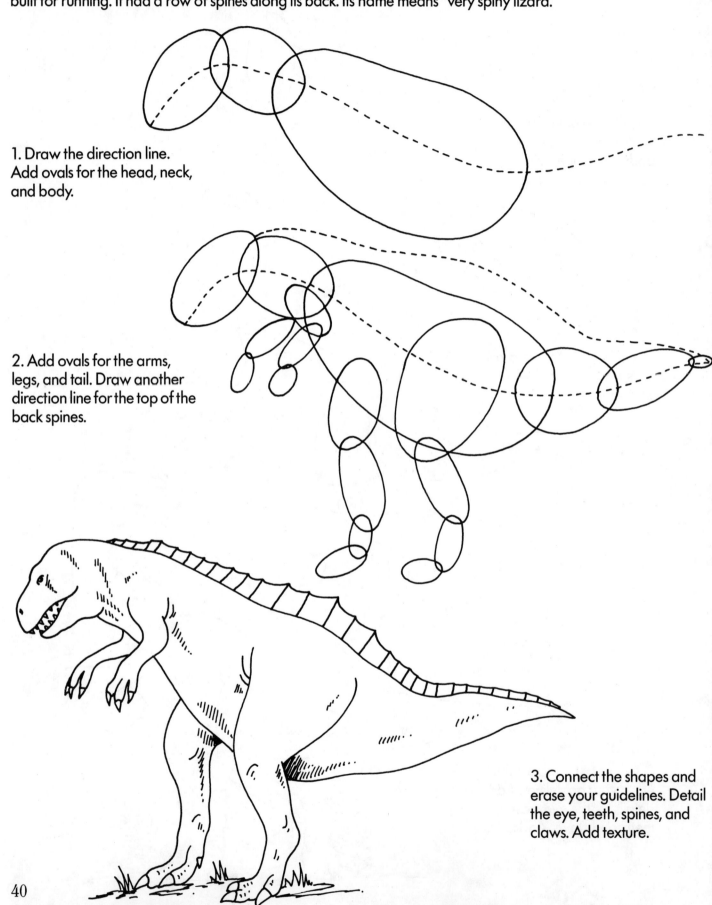

1. Draw the direction line. Add ovals for the head, neck, and body.

2. Add ovals for the arms, legs, and tail. Draw another direction line for the top of the back spines.

3. Connect the shapes and erase your guidelines. Detail the eye, teeth, spines, and claws. Add texture.

MONOCLONIUS

Monoclonius (mon-o-CLONE-ee-us) was a plant eater. The large horn on its nose was used to defend against enemies. The bony frill covering its neck was for protection from meat-eating creatures.

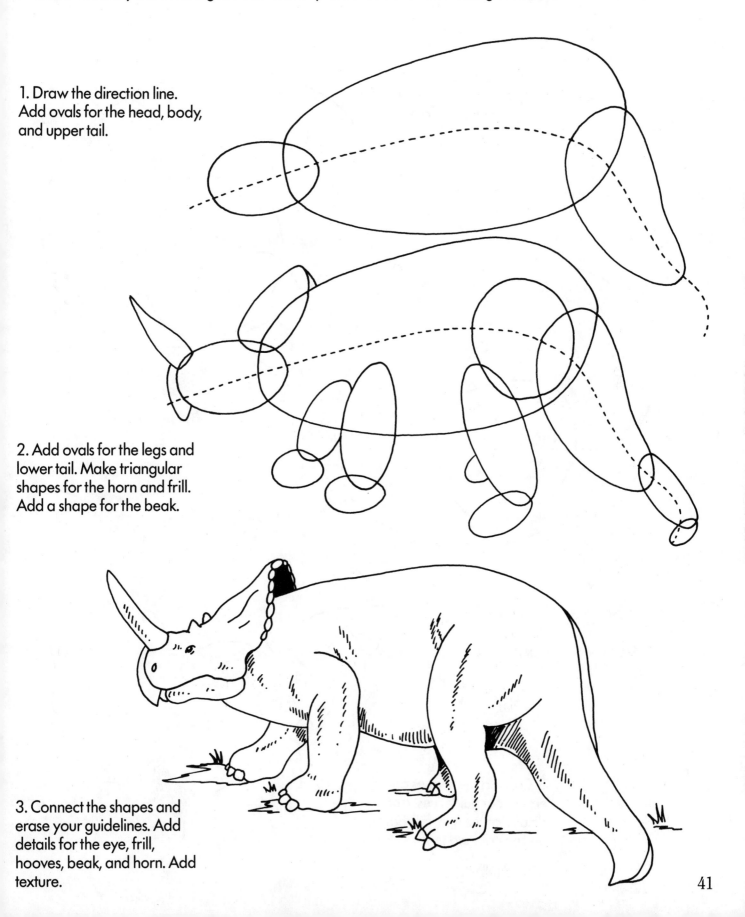

1. Draw the direction line. Add ovals for the head, body, and upper tail.

2. Add ovals for the legs and lower tail. Make triangular shapes for the horn and frill. Add a shape for the beak.

3. Connect the shapes and erase your guidelines. Add details for the eye, frill, hooves, beak, and horn. Add texture.

41

TRICERATOPS

Triceratops (try-SIR-uh-tops) means "three-horn-face." It also had a parrot-like beak and a huge bony frill over its neck. Let's practice drawing the head of the Triceratops first.

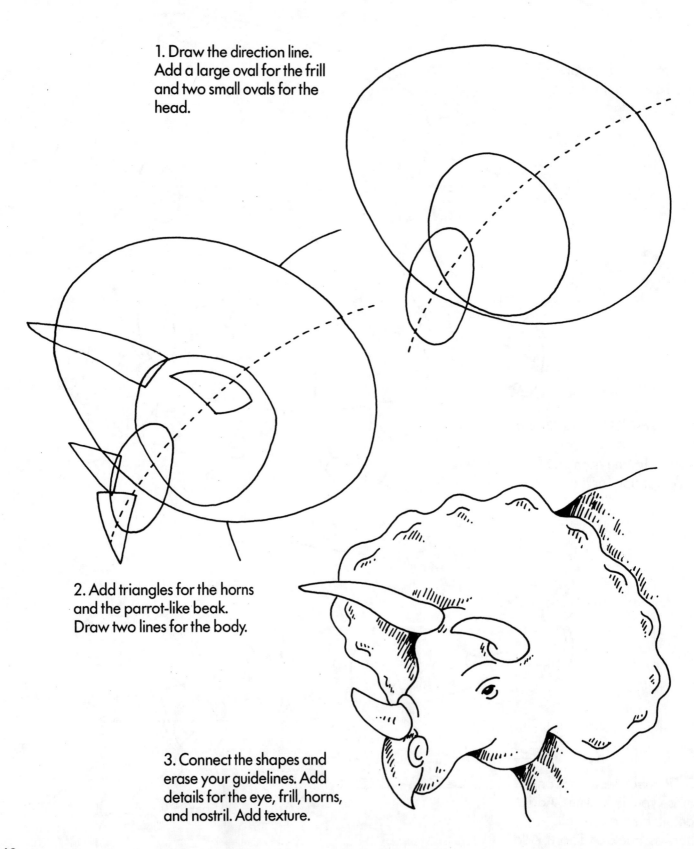

1. Draw the direction line. Add a large oval for the frill and two small ovals for the head.

2. Add triangles for the horns and the parrot-like beak. Draw two lines for the body.

3. Connect the shapes and erase your guidelines. Add details for the eye, frill, horns, and nostril. Add texture.

Now let's draw the full body of the Triceratops.

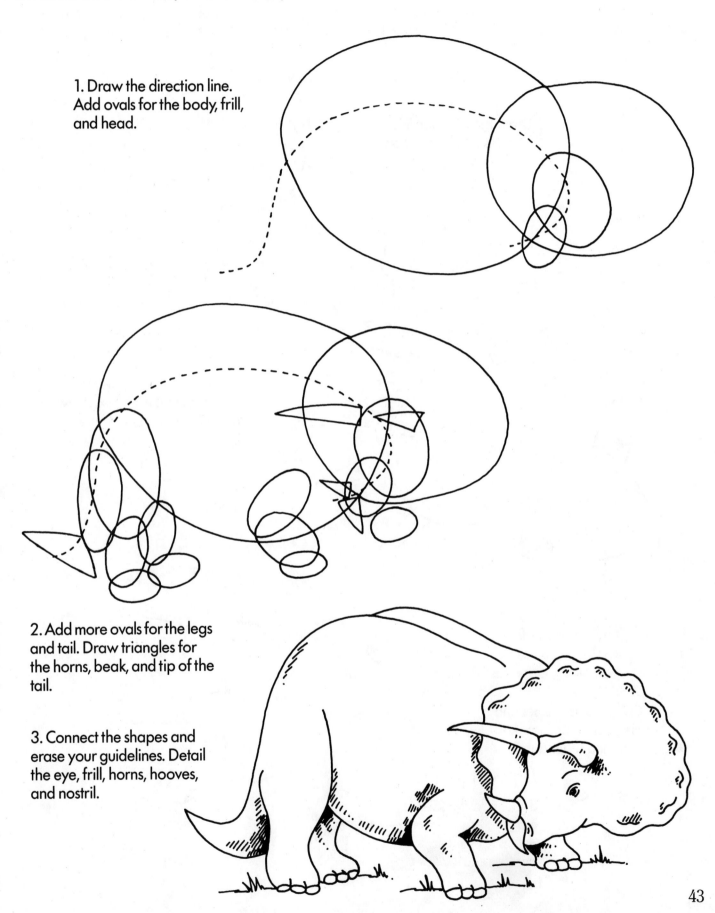

1. Draw the direction line. Add ovals for the body, frill, and head.

2. Add more ovals for the legs and tail. Draw triangles for the horns, beak, and tip of the tail.

3. Connect the shapes and erase your guidelines. Detail the eye, frill, horns, hooves, and nostril.

43

STYRACOSAURUS

A plant eater, Styracosaurus (sty-RAK-uh-sawr-us) grew as large as 19 feet long. Its most unusual feature was a large bony frill over its neck with six large spikes protruding from it. Styracosaurus also had a large horn growing out of its nose and a beak for a mouth. Let's draw the head of Styracosaurus first.

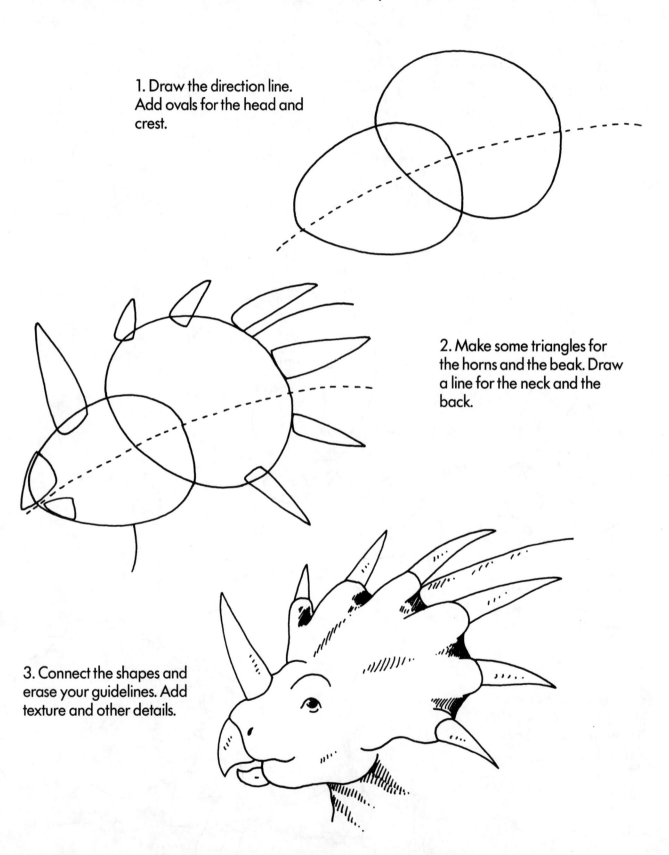

1. Draw the direction line. Add ovals for the head and crest.

2. Make some triangles for the horns and the beak. Draw a line for the neck and the back.

3. Connect the shapes and erase your guidelines. Add texture and other details.

Now let's draw the full body of Styracosaurus.

1. Draw the direction line. Add ovals for the body, head, and bony frill.

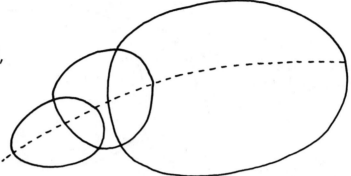

2. Add ovals for the legs and tail. Make triangles for the spikes and beak.

3. Connect the shapes and erase your guidelines. Detail the eye, nostril, spikes, and claws. Add texture.

SMILODON

Also known as the saber-toothed cat, Smilodon (SMY-luh-don) had two eight-inch-long fangs and powerful jaws. It was a fierce hunter.

1. Draw the direction line. Add ovals for the head, neck, and body.

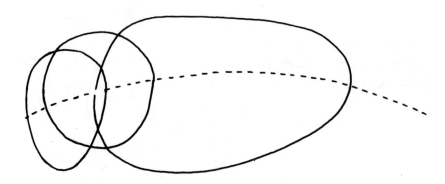

2. Add ovals for the legs and eyes. Draw triangles for the ears, nose, and fangs and two lines for the tail.

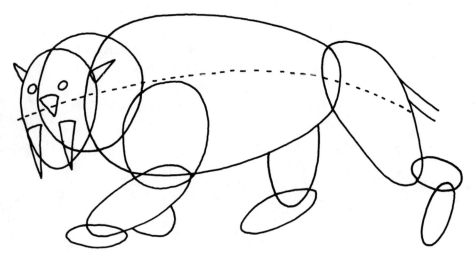

3. Connect the shapes and erase your guidelines. Add details to show the eyes, tongue, fangs, tail, and paws.

46

STEGOSAURUS

Stegosaurus (steg-uh-SAWR-us) was about the size of a large automobile. It was a plant eater with small, dull teeth. It was well protected by a unique row of bony plates along its back and four sharp spikes on its tail.

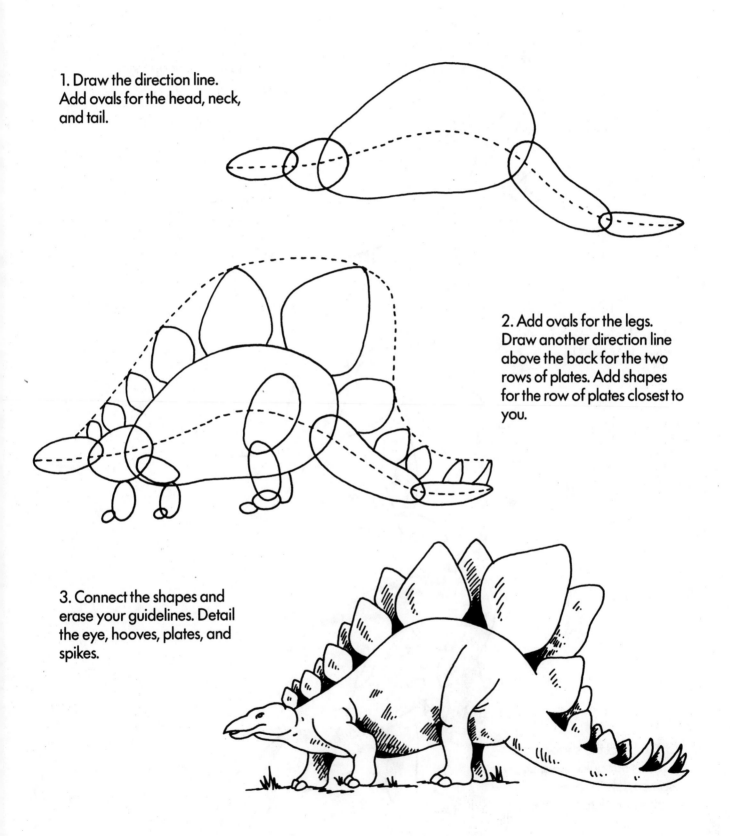

1. Draw the direction line. Add ovals for the head, neck, and tail.

2. Add ovals for the legs. Draw another direction line above the back for the two rows of plates. Add shapes for the row of plates closest to you.

3. Connect the shapes and erase your guidelines. Detail the eye, hooves, plates, and spikes.

PLATEOSAURUS

Plateosaurus (PLAY-tee-uh-sawr-us) was an early plant-eating dinosaur. It grew up to 20 feet long and weighed as much as a rhinoceros. Its front legs were short, but it could still walk on all fours.

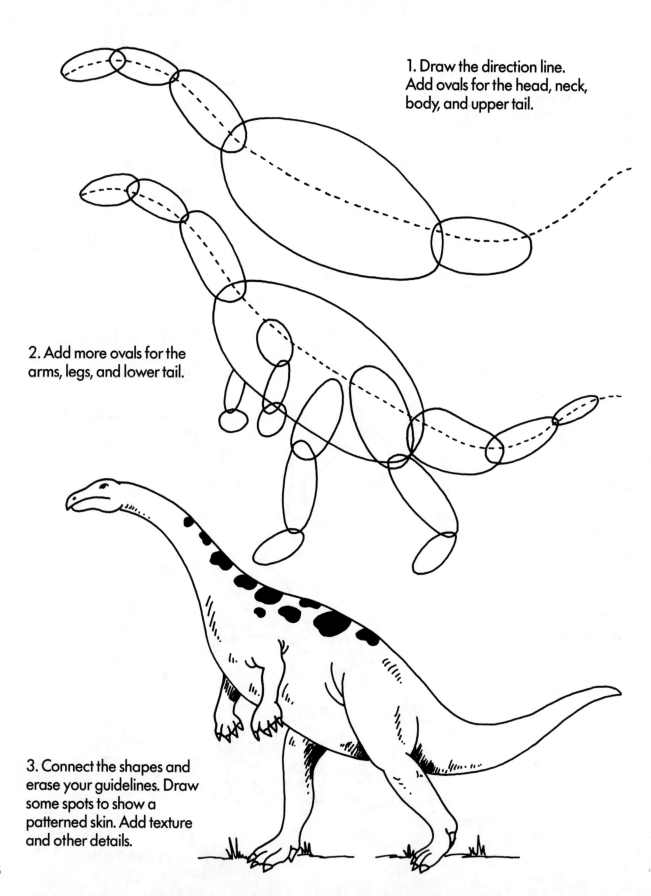

1. Draw the direction line. Add ovals for the head, neck, body, and upper tail.

2. Add more ovals for the arms, legs, and lower tail.

3. Connect the shapes and erase your guidelines. Draw some spots to show a patterned skin. Add texture and other details.

IGUANODON

Iguanodon (ig-WAN-o-don) weighed as much as three tons and stood as tall as 25 feet. It had sharp spiked thumbs.

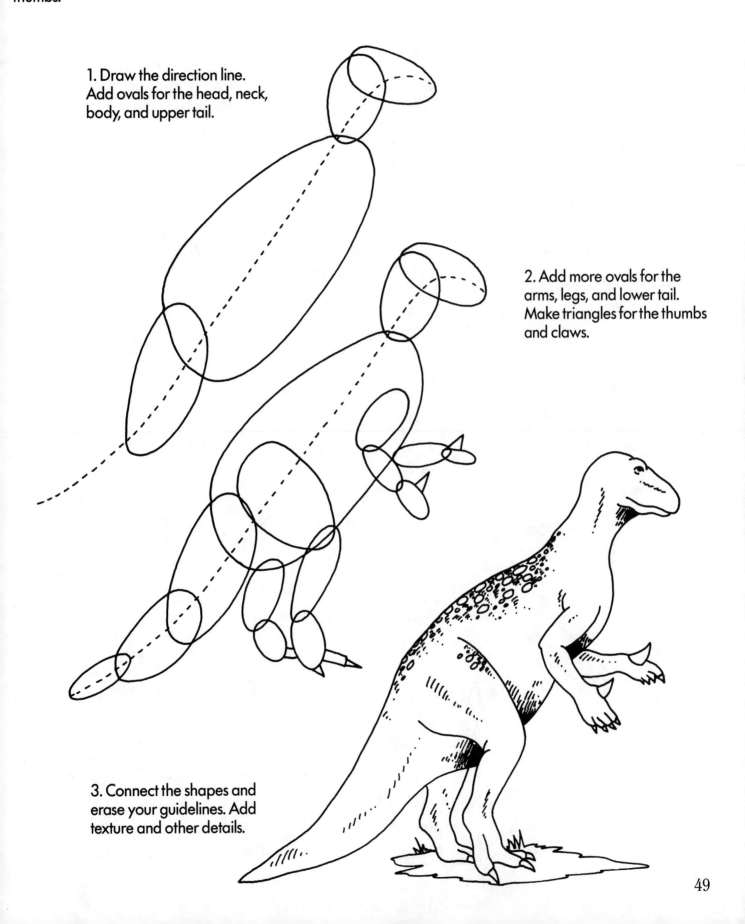

1. Draw the direction line. Add ovals for the head, neck, body, and upper tail.

2. Add more ovals for the arms, legs, and lower tail. Make triangles for the thumbs and claws.

3. Connect the shapes and erase your guidelines. Add texture and other details.

PARASAUROLOPHUS

Parasaurolophus (par-uh-sawr-OL-uh-fus) was a plant-eating dinosaur. The unusual crest on its head looked like a long tube with a knob on the end.

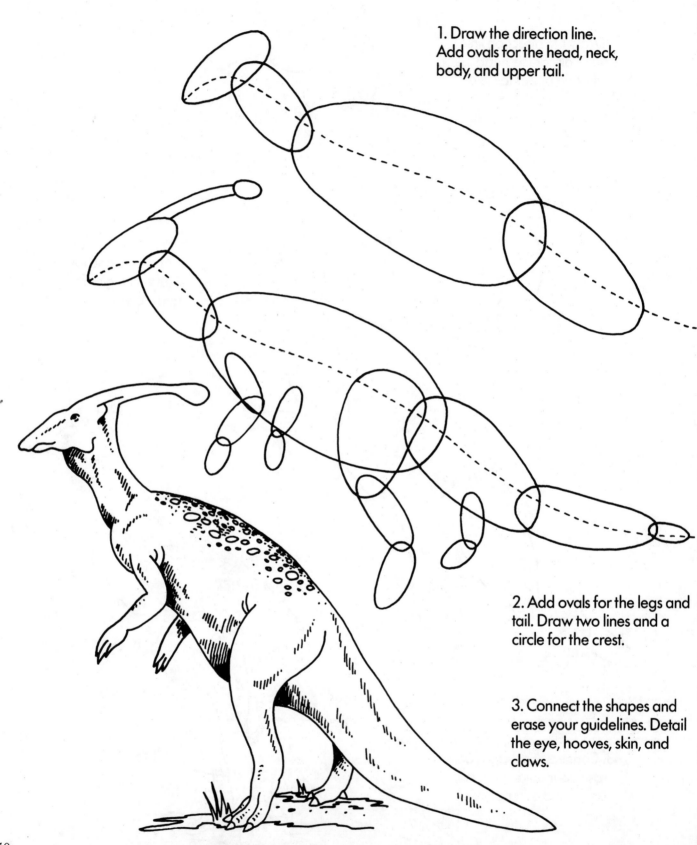

1. Draw the direction line. Add ovals for the head, neck, body, and upper tail.

2. Add ovals for the legs and tail. Draw two lines and a circle for the crest.

3. Connect the shapes and erase your guidelines. Detail the eye, hooves, skin, and claws.

50

TERATOSAURUS

One of the early meat-eating dinosaurs, Teratosaurus (ter-at-o-SAWR-us) had strong jaws, sharp teeth and claws, and large, powerful hind legs.

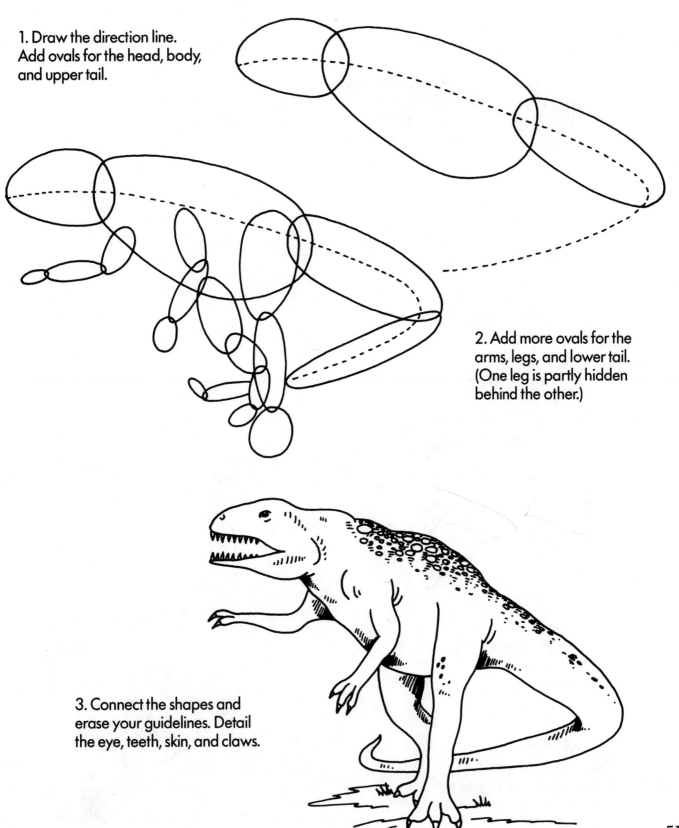

1. Draw the direction line. Add ovals for the head, body, and upper tail.

2. Add more ovals for the arms, legs, and lower tail. (One leg is partly hidden behind the other.)

3. Connect the shapes and erase your guidelines. Detail the eye, teeth, skin, and claws.

STENONYCHOSAURUS

Stenonychosaurus (sten-on-IK-uh-sawr-us) was a small meat-eating dinosaur with a triangular-shaped head. Scientists found fossils of this dinosaur along with groups of eggs.

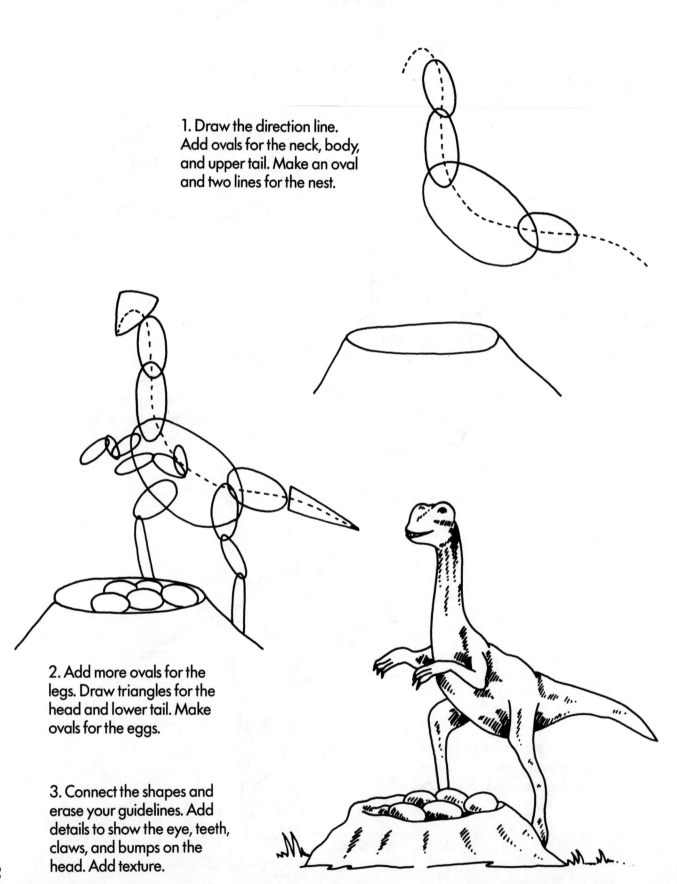

1. Draw the direction line. Add ovals for the neck, body, and upper tail. Make an oval and two lines for the nest.

2. Add more ovals for the legs. Draw triangles for the head and lower tail. Make ovals for the eggs.

3. Connect the shapes and erase your guidelines. Add details to show the eye, teeth, claws, and bumps on the head. Add texture.

UINTATHERIUM

Uintatherium (yoo-in-tuh-THEE-ree-um) was a huge plant eater that had four knob-shaped horns on its head. It was the biggest land mammal of its era.

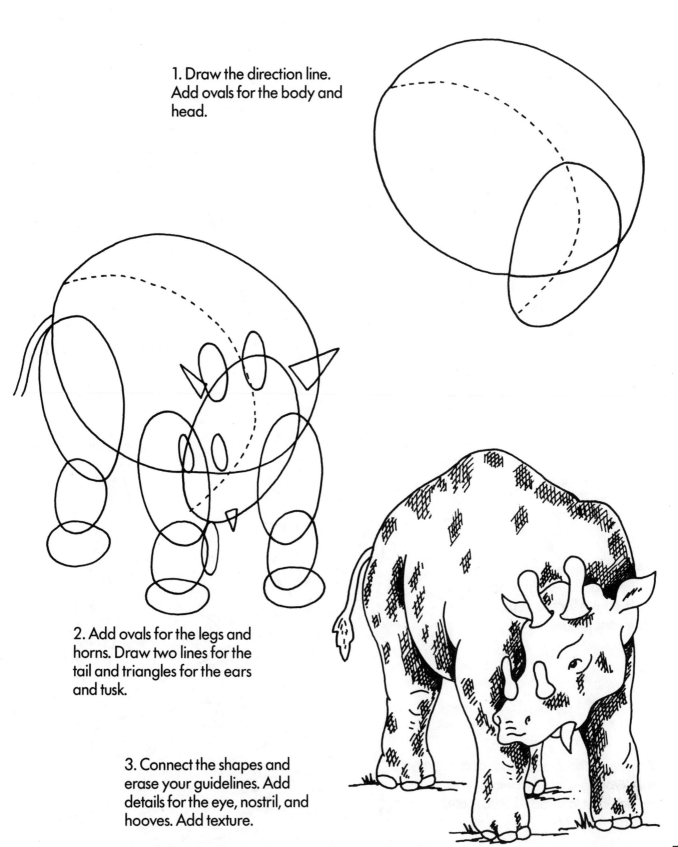

1. Draw the direction line. Add ovals for the body and head.

2. Add ovals for the legs and horns. Draw two lines for the tail and triangles for the ears and tusk.

3. Connect the shapes and erase your guidelines. Add details for the eye, nostril, and hooves. Add texture.

PTERANODON

Pteranodon (ter-AN-uh-don) was a flying reptile that lived during the time of the dinosaurs. Its name means "toothless wing."

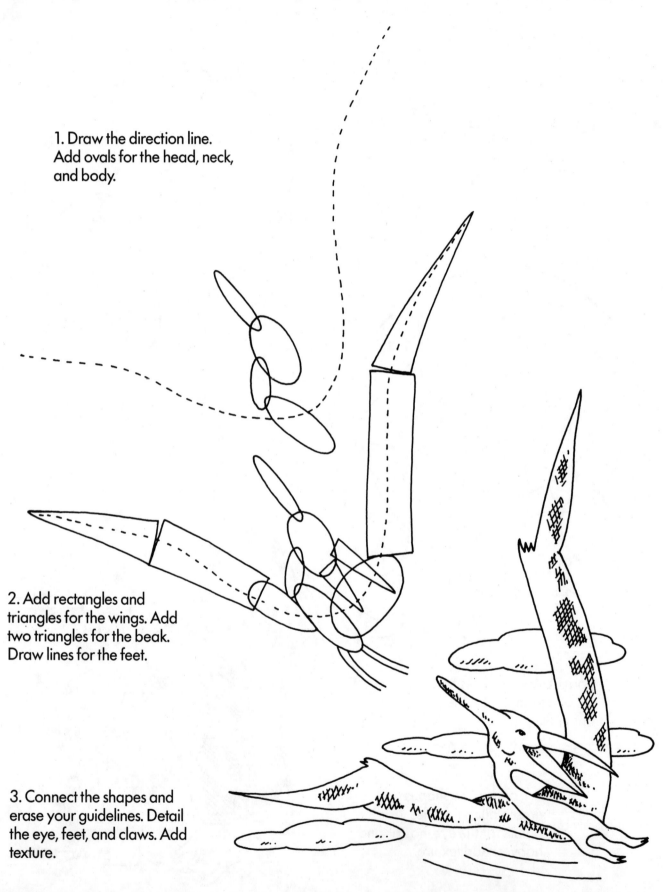

1. Draw the direction line. Add ovals for the head, neck, and body.

2. Add rectangles and triangles for the wings. Add two triangles for the beak. Draw lines for the feet.

3. Connect the shapes and erase your guidelines. Detail the eye, feet, and claws. Add texture.

RHAMPHORYNCUS

A flying reptile of the dinosaur era, Rhamphoryncus (ram-fuh-RINK-us) had sharp teeth and a wingspan of two feet. Its long tail had a flat piece on the end that helped it steer through the air.

1. Draw the direction line. Add ovals for the head, neck, and body. Draw lines for the legs.

2. Add two more direction lines for the wings. Make rectangles and triangles for the jaws and wing tips.

3. Connect the shapes and erase your guidelines. Detail the eye, teeth, and claws. Add texture.

DIMETRODON

Dimetrodon (dye-MET-ruh-don) was a meat-eating reptile that lived just before the time of the dinosaurs. It was as long as 10 feet and had fierce, knife-like teeth. The large sail on its back may have helped it control its body temperature.

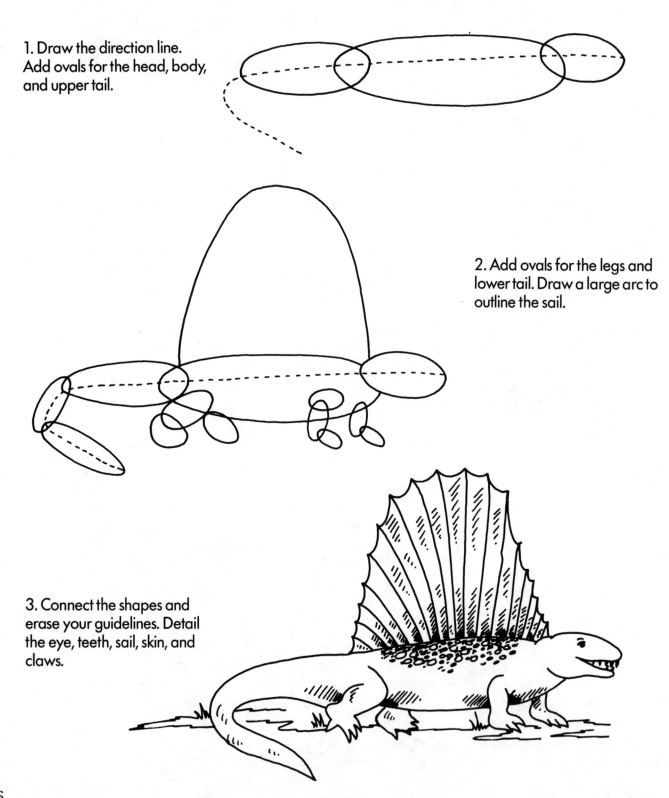

1. Draw the direction line. Add ovals for the head, body, and upper tail.

2. Add ovals for the legs and lower tail. Draw a large arc to outline the sail.

3. Connect the shapes and erase your guidelines. Detail the eye, teeth, sail, skin, and claws.

TYLOSAURUS

Tylosaurus (tie-loh-SAWR-us) was a giant reptile that lived in the seas during the time of the dinosaurs. It was as long as 20 feet and had a huge mouth filled with sharp teeth. It looked like a crocodile with flippers.

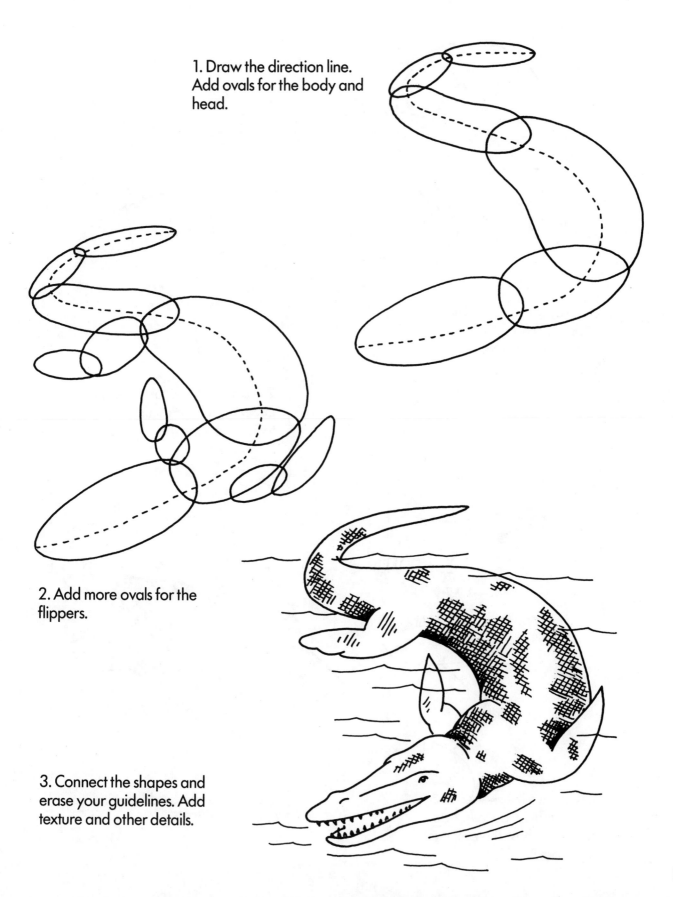

1. Draw the direction line. Add ovals for the body and head.

2. Add more ovals for the flippers.

3. Connect the shapes and erase your guidelines. Add texture and other details.

TYRANNOSAURUS

Tyrannosaurus (ty-ran-uh-SAWR-us) was one of the largest of the dinosaurs and certainly one of the scariest looking! It had a huge head and long, sharp teeth. Let's draw the head first.

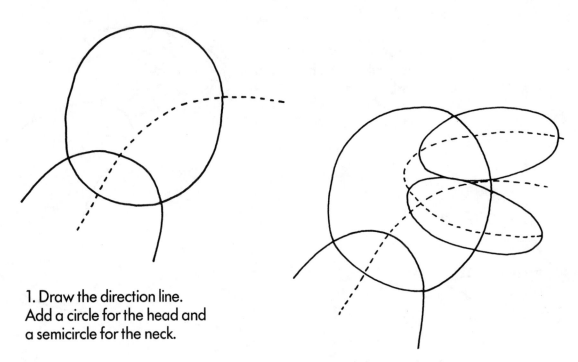

1. Draw the direction line. Add a circle for the head and a semicircle for the neck.

2. Add two ovals for the jaws. Draw another direction line to help position the upper and lower teeth.

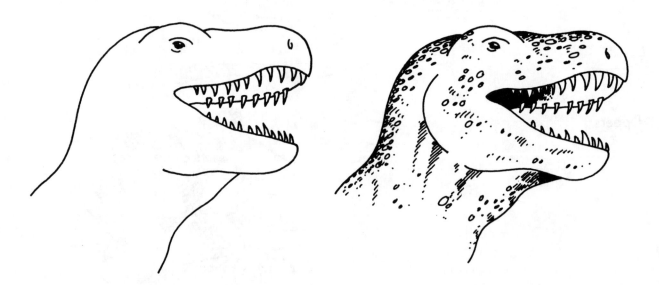

3. Connect the shapes and erase your guidelines. Add details to show the eye, teeth, and nostril.

4. Detail the skin. Add texture and other details.

Now let's draw the body of Tyrannosaurus.

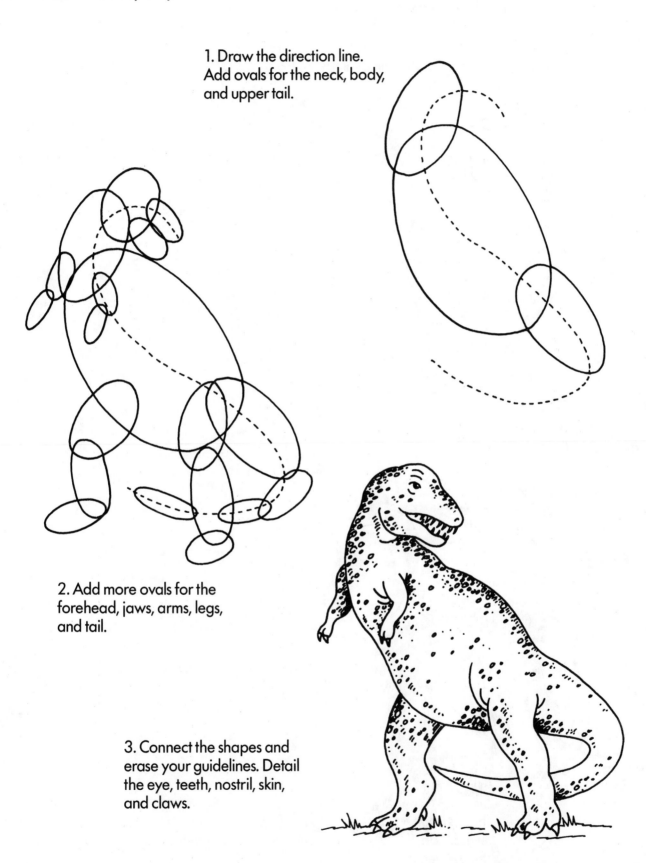

1. Draw the direction line. Add ovals for the neck, body, and upper tail.

2. Add more ovals for the forehead, jaws, arms, legs, and tail.

3. Connect the shapes and erase your guidelines. Detail the eye, teeth, nostril, skin, and claws.

WOOLLY MAMMOTH

The Woolly Mammoth (MAM-uth) was a relative of the elephant. They were very large, standing as tall as 14 feet. They had tremendous curved tusks. They lived during the Ice Age and had coats of long, thick fur.

1. Draw the direction line. Add an oval for the body.

2. Add ovals for the head, trunk, and legs. Draw more direction lines for the tusks.

3. Connect the shapes and erase your guidelines. Detail the eye, ear, tusks, and fur.

4. Add texture and other details.

CORYTHOSAURUS

Corythosaurus (Kor-ith-o-SAWR-us) was a duck-billed dinosaur. Its front jaw was wide and flat. On top of its head was a ridge of hollow bone that looked almost like a helmet.

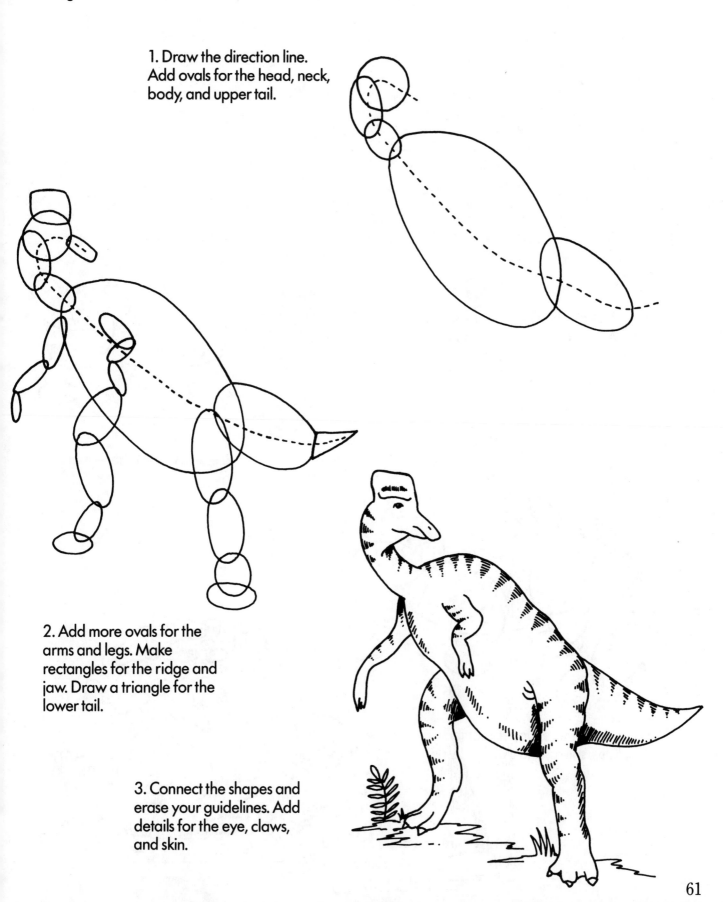

1. Draw the direction line. Add ovals for the head, neck, body, and upper tail.

2. Add more ovals for the arms and legs. Make rectangles for the ridge and jaw. Draw a triangle for the lower tail.

3. Connect the shapes and erase your guidelines. Add details for the eye, claws, and skin.

61

ANKYLOSAURUS

For protection from meat-eating dinosaurs, Ankylosaurus (an-kil-uh-SAWR-us) was covered with heavy armor plates. It had spikes on each side of its body and a club on its tail.

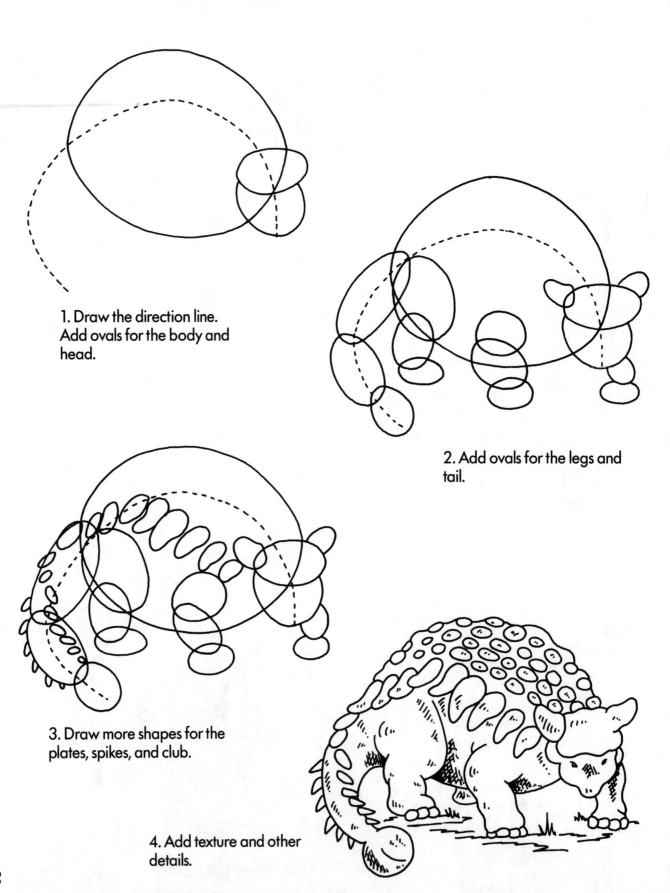

1. Draw the direction line. Add ovals for the body and head.

2. Add ovals for the legs and tail.

3. Draw more shapes for the plates, spikes, and club.

4. Add texture and other details.

GLYPTODON

Glyptodon (GLIP-to-don) was the ancestor of the armadillo. This huge mammal was as long as 10 feet and covered with a thick shell.

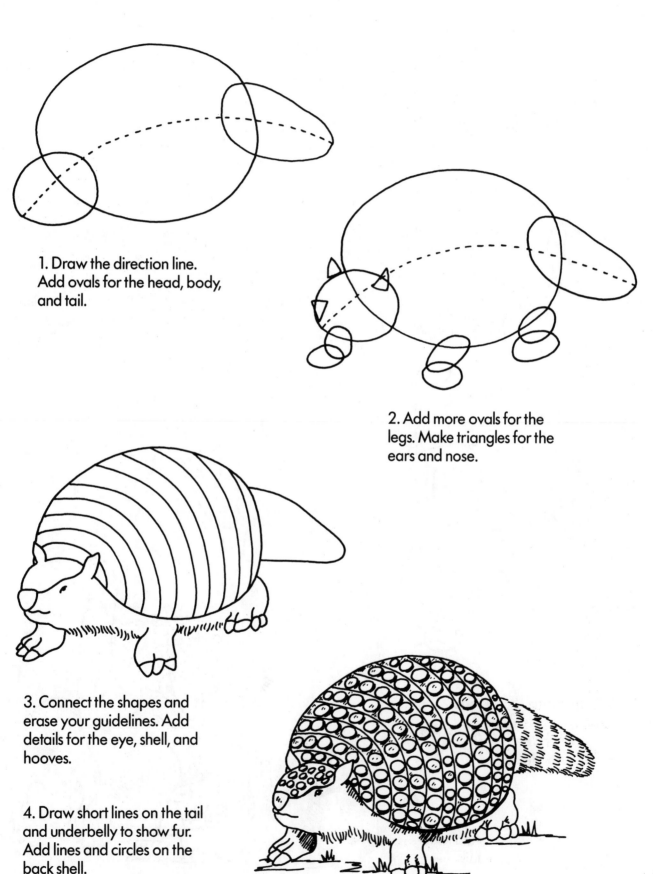

1. Draw the direction line. Add ovals for the head, body, and tail.

2. Add more ovals for the legs. Make triangles for the ears and nose.

3. Connect the shapes and erase your guidelines. Add details for the eye, shell, and hooves.

4. Draw short lines on the tail and underbelly to show fur. Add lines and circles on the back shell.

63

GROUPS OF DINOSAURS

Once you are able to draw individual dinosaurs, you may want to try drawing groups. Use the same technique of building up with direction lines and shapes. Start with the dinosaur that is closest to you and then add the dinosaurs behind it.

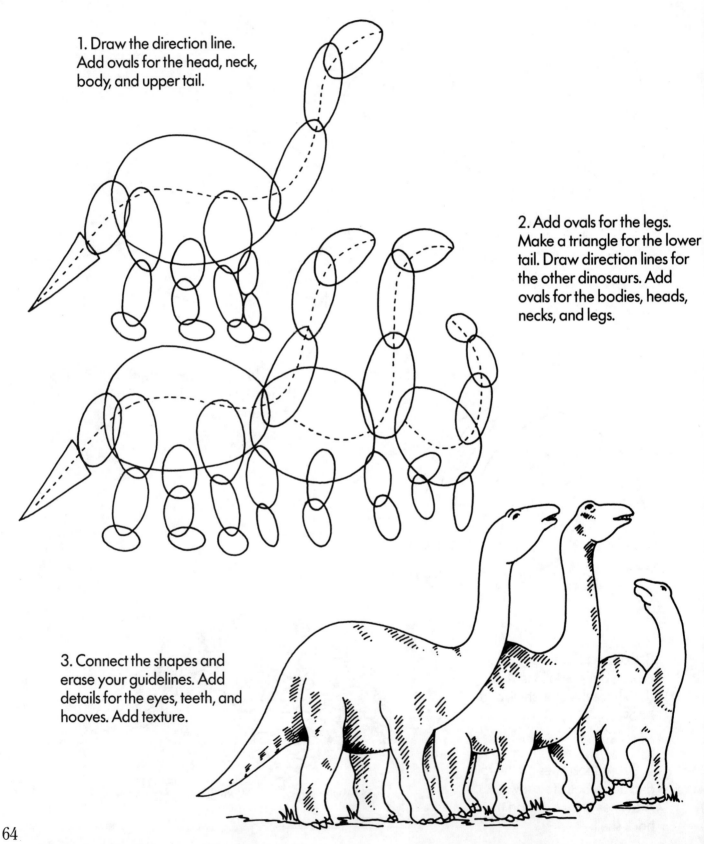

1. Draw the direction line. Add ovals for the head, neck, body, and upper tail.

2. Add ovals for the legs. Make a triangle for the lower tail. Draw direction lines for the other dinosaurs. Add ovals for the bodies, heads, necks, and legs.

3. Connect the shapes and erase your guidelines. Add details for the eyes, teeth, and hooves. Add texture.